The Tiniest Under the Railway

IRELAND'S ROYAL CANAL
1830 – 1899

Brian J. Goggin

RAILWAY & CANAL HISTORICAL SOCIETY

First published 2014
by the Railway & Canal Historical Society

www.rchs.org.uk

The Railway & Canal Historical Society was founded in 1954 and incorporated in 1967.
It is a company (No.922300) limited by guarantee and registered in England
as a charity (No.256047)
Registered office: 1–2 Vernon Street, Derby DE1 1FR

© Text Brian J. Goggin 2014 except chapter 7 © Ewan Duffy 2014

All rights reserved
No part of this publication may be reproduced or transmitted in any form
or by any means without the prior written permission of the publisher

ISBN 978 0 901461 61 2

Cover illustrations
*Two views of the lifting Effin Bridge in Dublin
front: with a pleasure boat passing under in 2014. Author
back: viewed though the remains of original 1st Lock – see p.54*

Designed and typeset by
Malcolm Preskett
Printed and bound in Great Britain by
Berforts Information Press
www.bookprinting.co.uk

Contents

Introduction   5

ONE   The Royal and Grand Canals   7

TWO   Sea ports, roads and markets   14

THREE   Some Royal Canal carriers   22

FOUR   Romance brought up the nine-fifteen   29

FIVE   Mallet's Insistent Pontoon   35

SIX   Steam in the 1870s   43

SEVEN   Royal Canal bridges in Dublin (Ewan Duffy)   51

EIGHT   Watson's Double Canal Boat   60

Notes and references   67

Acknowledgements

For illustrations and material, thanks to brightsolid Newspaper Archive Ltd [British Newspaper Archive], Euromapping, industrialheritageireland.info, the Institution of Civil Engineers, Ordnance Survey Ireland, the Railway Procurement Agency [RPA], the Waterways Archive [Canal and River Trust] and Waterways Ireland.

For their professionalism and especially for their patience in dealing with a novice, thanks to David Joy and Malcolm Preskett of R&CHS.

For Chapter 7 and for much useful comment on other chapters, thanks to Ewan Duffy; thanks also to Colin Becker for comments on the text.

Above all, thanks to Anne, the DBM.

bjg

A note on sources

Relatively little archive material was available to the authors of the two Royal Canal histories for the period from 1850 onwards. They were forced to rely for some information on evidence given, often many years after the event, to official enquiries. We have had the benefit of searchable online archives, which have made much more information accessible. Much of the new information in this book has come from contemporary newspaper accounts: the British Newspaper Archive http://www.britishnewspaperarchive.co.uk has been particularly useful. The online historic maps provided by Ordnance Survey Ireland http://maps.osi.ie neatly bookend our period and we are grateful to the Ordnance Survey for permission to use some extracts. The Enhanced Parliamentary Papers on Ireland site at http://www.dippam.ac.uk/eppi provides official documents and Messrs Google and others have kindly digitised, and made freely available, many 19th-century documents.

Introduction

The accounts of the Midland Great Western Railway for the half year ending 31 December 1849, four years after it bought the Royal Canal, showed its gross income from the railway as £23,773 and its income from the canal as £7,677, roughly a quarter of the total. By 1899, though, income from the railway was £264,393 and that from the canal £2,220, less than one per cent of the total. The Royal Canal, never particularly successful, had declined into utter irrelevance.

It may seem perverse, therefore, to offer even a short book on the canal's history in that period, especially as there exist two full histories, by Peter Clarke and by Ruth Delany (with Ian Bath in the most recent edition). This, though, is not a full history, even of the limited period, roughly 1830–1899, from just before the railway took over until the end of the nineteenth century. This is rather a complement to those histories, providing just enough background information to enable the book to stand alone while covering some new topics and providing new or extra information on others. The topics include:

— the 120-foot steam-powered narrowboat;
— the Midland Great Western Railway's early attempts at running canal boats;
— the ingenious Mr Mallet's moveable bridge;
— the whore who held the mortgage on the canal;
— the competition between the roads of Roscommon and the Royal Canal;
— the reconstruction of Dublin bridges over the canal;
— the horses who slept on board their boat.

I am particularly grateful to Ewan Duffy for allowing the inclusion of the result of his researches into the reconstruction of Royal Canal bridges in Dublin.

But this book is not intended to be the last word on any of those topics. I hope that it might encourage others – those researching local, family, social, industrial, transport, economic or technological history – to record and transmit anything they might learn about the history of the Royal Canal. To take just three topics, we know very little about canal employees, the operations of canal traders or the management of the horse-drawn canal boats. On any one of those, useful information could just as easily be found by a local or family historian as by a canal specialist.

> *the most interesting thing in the world is to find out how the next man gets his vittles.**

Brian J. Goggin, July 2014

---

* Kipling (from 'Captains Courageous')

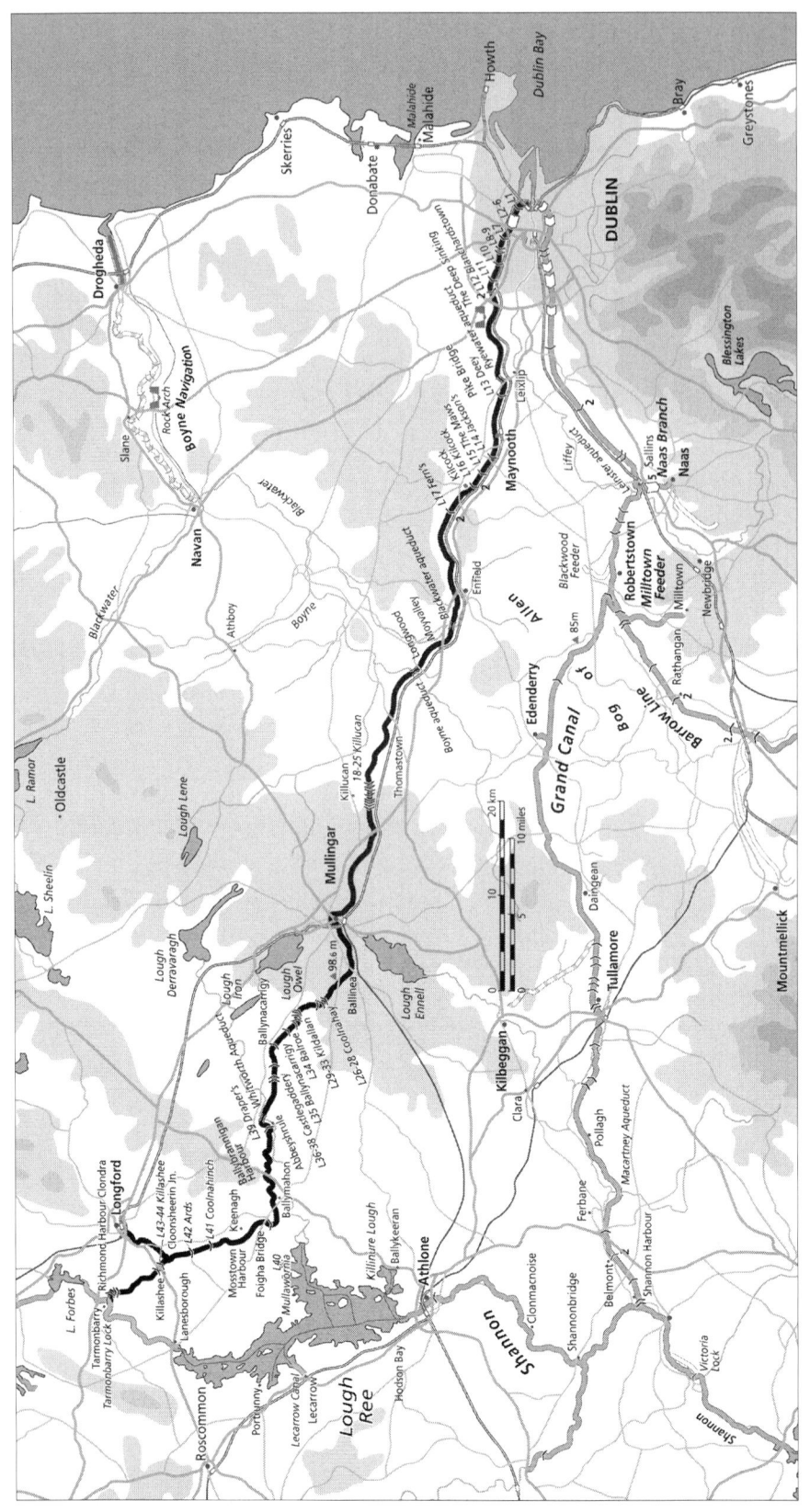

The Royal Canal, linking the river Shannon to Dublin and the Irish Sea

© *Euromapping 2014*

ONE

The Royal and Grand Canals

THE river Shannon runs roughly from north to south through the flat midlands of Ireland. The river is linked by two canals to Dublin on the east coast. The Grand Canal runs from the south side of Dublin to join the Shannon near Banagher, on the stretch of river between the two large lakes of Lough Ree and Lough Derg. The Royal Canal runs from the north side of Dublin to join the Shannon near Tarmonbarry and Longford, upstream of Lough Ree. Both canals were begun in the latter part of the 18th century and reached the Shannon in the early 19th.

The Royal Canal, from the river Liffey in Dublin to the river Shannon, is about 90 miles long, with 46 locks, 10 of which are doubles (staircase pairs). It had two lockless spurs, one to Broadstone in Dublin and the other, near the western end, to the town of Longford. It was officially closed to navigation in 1961 but (apart from the spurs) has since been restored – the final stretch was reopened in 2010.

The navigation authority, Waterways Ireland, gives these navigation dimensions on its website:

Length of locks	21 m	(68 feet 11 inches)
Beam of locks	3.9 m	(12 feet 10 inches)
Draft	1 m	(3 feet 3 inches)

'given as a guide only and cannot be guaranteed'[1]

The Royal and the Grand

IN 1836 His late Majesty William the Fourth, by the Grace of God, of the United Kingdom of Great Britain and Ireland, King, Defender of the Faith, appointed Commissioners 'to consider and recommend a general system of railways for Ireland'. The Commissioners' first report, in 1837, said that work was under way; their second, delivered in 1838 to King William's successor Queen Victoria, was much longer and, in its many appendices, assembled a large amount of information about traffic and travel in Ireland at the time.[2]

The report's Appendix B No.6 gives 'Returns relating to inland navigations in

TABLE 1: Irish navigations – Tonnage carried

Navigation	length (miles) [3]	year	tons carried
River Suir (Carrick-on-Suir to Clonmel)	13	—	3,000
Tyrone (Lough Neagh to Coalisland)	12	1836	7,291
Upper Shannon (Lough Ree to Lough Allen)	59	1835	9,770
Lower Boyne (Drogheda to Carrickdexter)	13	1836	10,195
Limerick Navigation (Limerick to Killaloe)	15	1836	36,018
Lagan (Belfast to Lough Neagh)	28	1836	44,700
River Slaney (Wexford to Enniscorthy)	18	—	60,000
River Barrow (tidal lock to Athy)	43	1835	66,085
Royal Canal (including branches). Tonnage excludes 36,002 pigs, 7,639 casks of butter	99	1836	88,334
Newry Canal (Newry to Lough Neagh)	17	1836	102,770
Grand Canal (including branches). Tonnage includes cattle and pigs. About 20,000 tons of this was carried from the Shannon to Dublin	164	1837	215,911

Compiled from Appendix B No.6 of the Second Report of the Railway Commissioners

TABLE 2: Irish navigations – toll income

Navigation	year	tolls (£) [4]
River Suir (Carrick-on-Suir to Clonmel)	—	—
Tyrone (Lough Neagh to Coalisland)	—	—
Upper Shannon (Lough Ree to Lough Allen)	1835	100
Lower Boyne (Drogheda to Carrickdexter)	1837	707
Limerick Navigation (Limerick to Killaloe)	1836	1,514
Lagan (Belfast to Lough Neagh)	1836	2,061
River Slaney (Wexford to Enniscorthy)	—	—
River Barrow (tidal lock to Athy)	1835	4,966
Royal Canal (including branches)	1836	13,095
Newry Canal (Newry to Lough Neagh)	1837	3,506
Grand Canal (including branches)	1837	37,557

Compiled from Appendix B No.6 of the Second Report of the Railway Commissioners

TABLE 3: Irish navigations – passenger traffic

Navigation	year	passengers
Middle Shannon (steamer; Killaloe to Shannon Harbour)	— [5]	4,083
Limerick Navigation (horse-drawn; Limerick to Killaloe)	1836	14,600
Royal Canal	1837	46,450
Grand Canal	1836	88,364

Compiled from Appendix B No 6 of the Second Report of the Railway Commissioners

Ireland'. There are inconsistencies in the way the returns are compiled and presented for different navigations, but they nonetheless provide a useful picture of traffic in the mid 1830s. They show that the Grand Canal was the busiest navigation in Ireland, whether that was measured by tonnage carried (TABLE 1), by toll income (TABLE 2), or by numbers of passengers carried (TABLE 3)

Why was the Grand so much more successful than the Royal? This chapter and the next attempt to answer that question.

Passenger traffic

THE Royal and Grand Canal companies both carried passengers in horse-drawn passage boats. There was no passenger service on the upper Shannon, where the Royal Canal met the river, and the canal passage boats did not travel further than the nearby town of Longford. The Grand Canal service connected, at Shannon Harbour, with the steamers operated by the Inland Steam Navigation Company 'connected with the City of Dublin Steam Packet Company'. The steamers provided a scheduled service on the river Shannon; they connected in turn at Killaloe, at the downstream end of Lough Derg, with the horse-drawn passage boat of the Limerick Navigation Company; from Limerick steamers were available to carry passengers on the Shannon estuary.

In 1836 the Royal Canal Company earned £7,468 from its passenger services, with an additional £519 from carrying parcels; the Grand Canal Company did not state the total income.[6]

Both companies invested in fast boats for daytime service. The Grand Canal Company said

The Swift Passage Boats were established in June, 1835, when the Fares were considerably reduced. They are generally 60 feet in length and 6 feet in breadth, and are designed to accommodate 20 first-cabin, and 32 second-cabin passengers, together with the master and crew, though not unfrequently they carry a larger number, and travel at the rate of 10 British miles an hour, between locks ... The night boats, 60 feet long and 8 feet broad, are designed to carry 45 first-cabin and 35 second-cabin passengers, and to travel at the rate of 6 British miles an hour.[7]

However, the Royal Canal Company was first in Ireland to introduce the fast boats. It announced in September 1833 that it was 'making preliminary arrangements for plying their newly invented passage boats, by which double the speed of their present boats in the same time will be attained, without any application of increased power'.[8] In December, the company announced '*UNPRECEDENTED SPEED ATTAINED IN TRAVELLING UPON THE ROYAL CANAL*' and said that its 70-passenger iron boat, built in Scotland,[9] would leave Dublin at 9am and reach Mullingar, 53 miles away, at 5pm.[10] By 1837 the service was even faster, reaching Mullingar at 4.30pm and passing, *en route*, a similar boat coming in the other direction. The company also operated slower night-boats: one left Dublin each day at 3pm and reached Longford, 91 miles away, at 9am next day, while another left Longford at 1pm and reached Dublin at 7am.

Horse-drawn cars met both day and night boats:

Mr Bianconi runs Two-Horse Cars, in conjunction with the Night Boats, to and from <u>Glasson</u>, <u>Athlone</u>, <u>Lanesborough</u>, Roscommon, Castlerea, Newtownforbes, <u>Rooskey</u>, <u>Drumod</u>, <u>Drumsna</u>, <u>Jamestown</u>, <u>Carrick-on-Shannon</u>, and Boyle; and there are Cars also to run to and from Elphin and Strokestown ... A Car likewise runs in conjunction with the Day Boats to and from Edgeworthstown and Mullingar.[11]

The towns which have been underlined were all on the east bank of the river Shannon but their links to the canal were by road, not by water.

In 1845 the canal was bought by the Midland Great Western Railway of Ireland [MGWR] and by 1848 the railway had reached Mullingar.[12] In December 'eight (iron) canal passage boats' were put up for auction at the Royal Canal Dockyard in Dublin: 'To the Purchasers every facility will be afforded either for the Repairing or Breaking up of said Boats'.[13]

The Grand Canal Company's last canal passage boat ceased carrying in 1852.[14] The era of canal passenger-carrying had ended.

The Middle Shannon and the Grand

THE horse-drawn cars that met the passage boats illustrate an important point about the Royal Canal: its relationship with the Shannon was entirely different from that between the Grand Canal and the river.

The Grand Canal's junction with the river, at Shannon Harbour, is in the middle of nowhere. The nearest town of any significance, and the nearest bridge across the Shannon, are at Banagher, about two miles downstream. In 1806, the Grand Canal Company leased the Middle Shannon from the Directors General of Inland Navigation. That gave the company control of the river section between Lough Derg and Lough Ree, in other words between the towns of Portumna and Athlone. The company hoped to attract traffic from the Shannon on to the canal and, by 1817, there were 26 boats trading between the river and Dublin. However, tracking (towing from the shore) was impossible on the Shannon: boats had to be poled on river sections and sailed on the lakes.[15]

The introduction of steamers increased the traffic from the Shannon to the Grand Canal. The Grand Canal Company gave special rates to the Inland Steam Navigation Company (later subsumed into the City of Dublin Steam Packet Company) on goods carried to the canal. The steam company's vessels did carry passengers, but their primary role was as tugs: they hauled laden barges ('lumber boats' or 'trade boats') north from Lough Derg and south from Athlone to the Grand Canal.

In 1835 the steam company had one vessel, the iron 12hp 101-ton steamer *Marquis Wellesley*, based in Athlone. In that year it went to Shannon Harbour once very three days; altogether it hauled 130 boats carrying a total of 3,993 tons. The company also had two large steamers on Lough Derg; they were unable to travel upstream of Portumna, so they handed over passengers and the towing of trade boats to two smaller steamers, both of iron, each of 103 tons: the *Avonmore* of 24 hp and the *Dunally* of 18 hp. In 1835 they hauled 467 boats, carrying a total of 15,482 tons, north from Portumna.[16] Thus in 1835 the Grand Canal received almost 20,000 tons from Lough Derg and from Athlone, in addition to whatever was generated along the Portumna–Athlone stretch, the 'middle Shannon'.[17]

The Upper Shannon and the Royal

THERE was no such feeder service to the Royal Canal. Steamers ventured only occasionally north of Athlone on to Lough Ree; indeed trading vessels of any kind were scarce.

In 1832 Thomas Rhodes CE, reporting on the state of the river Shannon, highlighted the problems caused by the 'peculiar form, devious course and nature of the great line of the Shannon navigation, its lakes and broad waters'. Sailing boats could make headway only with a fair wind and on a direct course; towing from the land was impossible in many places because the shallow, reedy banks would have required very long lines; it would have been impracticable in floods. Boats were therefore rowed with sweeps [long oars], pushed along with 'sett poles' or towed by small pulling-boats:

and as all these several methods are very slow and tardy, even in calm weather, but with adverse winds, and prevailing as they do from the west a great portion of the year, detains vessels bound from the Upper Shannon to Dublin and Limerick many weeks on their voyage, which makes it expensive, and in some cases (from the nature of the cargo) this detention proves a loss both to the merchant and owner of the vessel.[18]

In 1837 Commander James Wolfe RN, surveying Lough Ree for the Admiralty, wrote:

This lake is but little used in a commercial way, not a trading vessel of any description crosses its surface, and even the boats for carrying turf, which are occasionally seen passing to and fro, merely supply the islands or other places where this necessary article cannot be more easily obtained ... There are, however, the two points to which the produce of the surrounding country is sent for shipment to Dublin; from Athlone by the Grand Canal, and from Lanesborough [at the northern end of the lake] by the Royal Canal. From the latter place, lumber boats adapted to canal navigation are poled or sailed up to Cloondara [Clondra], a distance of seven English miles, to the junction of the Royal Canal with the Shannon; but at Athlone a small steamer is employed to tow the boats twice a-week to and from Shannon Harbour, where the Grand Canal enters the river.[19]

While taking their soundings and creating their charts, the Admiralty surveyors also sketched both Lough Derg and Lough Ree. Several of their drawings of Lough Derg show steamers, but those of Lough Ree show only a few small boats.[20]

Isaac Weld on the Upper Shannon

BUT the most eloquent account of the problems of the upper Shannon was provided by Isaac Weld. He was born in Dublin in 1774 and, at the age of 21, he sailed to Philadelphia and spent two years touring north America, where he met (amongst others) George Washington. He returned in 1797 'without entertaining the slightest wish to revisit the American continent' and later navigated the Lakes of Killarney in a boat he made from compressed brown paper.[21] In 1815 a 14hp paddle-steamer, originally called *Argyle* but renamed *Thames*, visited Dublin *en route* from Clydeside to London on one of the earliest steam sea voyages in these islands; Weld persuaded Captain Dodd to take him and his wife as the only passengers on the fifteen-day voyage to London.[22]

As Honorary Secretary of the Royal Dublin Society, Weld helped to set up the programme of Statistical Surveys of Irish counties; he himself wrote the survey of County Roscommon.[23] That county occupies most of the west bank of the river Shannon from Shannonbridge, downstream of Athlone, upriver to the southern section of Lough Allen. Weld's work included an account of each section of the Shannon and an investigation of the flows of trade by river, canal and road. The Shannon end of the Royal Canal was just across the river in County Longford; Weld's survey helps to explain why the Royal Canal did not attract more of County Roscommon's trade.

Weld pointed out that there were only three quays: one at Carrick-on-Shannon, one of 120ft at Drumsna and the Irish Mining Company's coal quay on Lough Allen. He quoted Charles Wye Williams, of the steam company, on the deficiencies of the infrastructure:

the almost total want of those essentials and conveniences for trading, without which it is comparatively useless, viz shelter-harbours, piers, quays and landing-places, landmarks and beacons ... [the lack of] cranes, weighing machines, well-appointed boats and barges, stores conveniently situated, tackle of all sorts, and the thousand aids and contrivances which human skill has devised for expediting business ... On the entire 500 miles of coast of the Shannon, there was not, twelve months back, a single crane; an article which, in England, is as common as a waggon or an anchor.[24]

Merchants in Boyle told Weld that they rarely used the Shannon, and only for heavy goods that, with no warehouses, 'would withstand bad weather and rough treatment'. Although Carrick-on-Shannon was close to Boyle, and linked to it by a good road, the smaller, more distant town of Drumsna acted as Boyle's Shannon port because navigation between Carrick and Drumsna was so difficult. Weld was told that, at times during the 'shipping season', Drumsna was crowded with drays and cars, but it had no stores or warehouses. Corn was tipped direct from cars into boats; if supply exceeded the capacity of the available boats, private houses were hired for storage. (Tipping from cars to boats was also used at Lanesborough but boats could be loaded only in dry weather.)

Downstream, at the small town of Rooskey, a canal carried the navigation past the shallows and a bridge carried a road across the river; Weld said 'it comes in for a participation of the trade on the river'.

Downstream again, the next bridge was at Tarmonbarry. The Royal Canal's Shannon terminus, Richmond Harbour, was nearby, on the east side of the Shannon at Clondra. The harbour had a dry dock and warehouses; boats leaving the harbour locked down into the Camlin River and then passed through a short canal, with one lock, into the Shannon just below Tarmonbarry.

There was another short canal to avoid shoals at Lanesborough, at the head of Lough Ree. It had a small basin in which boats had been sunk to preserve them from the sun until they were needed for the next corn-shipping season. There were some old stores nearby. The innkeeper owned four boats but had sent them for repair, not to the dry dock at Richmond Harbour but all the way to Mullingar, which suggested a lack of boatbuilders on the upper Shannon.

Lough Ree had unmarked rocks and shoals and its depth varied with the seasons: rocks that were covered in winter were near the surface in summer – but at least some of them could then be seen. Canal boats were not usually suitable for sailing but some boats had 'moveable masts'; they sailed only in favourable winds. They used poles on the river sections but soft mud bottoms made that difficult. There was no public quay on either side of the lake and loading and unloading were difficult; there were only two public roads leading to the shore and there were no villages. Few cargoes were delivered to or collected from around the lake and Weld only once saw a 'boat of burthen upon its waters'. A steamer had been brought to Athlone to tow boats on the lake but there was no demand for its services. The only regular traffic was of coal from Lough Allen brought downstream, although that coal was not used by Athlone's breweries or distilleries or by the steamers downriver. Weld wrote of the upper Shannon traffic in general:

But along the shores of Roscommon, with the exception of the one article of coals, nature has dispensed her bounties with such an even hand, and the population is so much dispersed over the face of the country, that interchange in native commodities of the first necessity is on too limited a scale, to require the aid of the large boats in use for commerce; and as for small market boats, or for local purposes, similar to what are seen on lakes and rivers in some other countries, these are quite unknown on the upper Shannon.

The river Shannon had its deficiencies as a navigation, but that was not enough to explain why the western end of the Royal Canal did not receive more traffic from the surrounding counties. Weld provided more information about traffic flows: his account continues in Chapter 2.

TWO

Sea ports, roads and markets

THE Royal Canal provided a route from County Roscommon, and other Shannon counties, to Dublin and its port. Isaac Weld described the nature of the traffic on the canal.

The trade in connexion with the canals, consists principally in corn and butter for exportation, and in heavy and bulky articles from Dublin in return, such as sugars, iron, deals, slates, earthenware, and British manufactured goods generally…
The communication by water between Richmond harbour and Dublin, along the canal, is frequent and regular: four merchant boats start in each week on fixed days; but the passage boats proceed no farther than the town of Longford, distant five miles.

The competition from road traffic

HOWEVER, Weld emphasised that Dublin was not the only port available to Roscommon. Nowhere in the county was further than 40 miles from Sligo or Galway, whose traders competed with those of Dublin to supply the county with timber and iron and to export its corn. Communications with all three ports were good and Roscommon people knew where the best prices were: 'Trade is seldom long in finding its true level and most advantageous channel'.

There was a daily stage from Roscommon to Killashee on the Royal Canal 'whence passage boats afford a cheap and ready conveyance to Dublin'; there were also daily stage cars to Athlone, from which there was a choice of coaches that reached Dublin in only eight to nine hours.

There were two excellent mail-coach roads through the county. One, from Dublin to Sligo, crossed the Shannon at Carrick and went through Boyle, the main market town in the north of the county; the other, from Dublin to Galway, crossed the Shannon at Athlone and went through Ballinasloe in the south of the county. Another road was being built from Longford on the east side of the Shannon: it would cross at Tarmonbarry and run through the county to Westport in County Mayo.[25] Market information was readily available and coaches could carry 'the lighter and more valuable goods for the shops'.

Heavier goods could be carried by cars or drays and cattle could be walked to the markets and to the ports. The locations of the markets influenced the flows of produce: land on the Roscommon side of the river near Tarmonbarry was good for growing wheat – but that wheat was not sent to Richmond Harbour, across the river, for transport to Dublin. It went instead to the market at Strokestown, six miles away, where it was sold to merchants from Sligo, 38 miles away, for export through their port.[26] The impediment to the use of the Royal was not the prices offered but the 'infamous' condition of the road between Strokestown and Tarmonbarry. Similarly, the road from Roscommon town to the Shannon at Lanesborough was 'by an extraordinary instance of perverseness or neglect ... suffered to remain in a most reprehensible state'.

Thus the Royal Canal and Dublin faced competition from Sligo for the trade of Boyle (20 miles away), Carrick-on-Shannon (7½ more) and Drumsna (10 more) as well as Tarmonbarry and Strokestown. Galway competed with Dublin and Sligo for the trade of Lanesborough; Athlone was midway between the two canals to Dublin but only 40 miles by coach road from Galway.

At an average cost for land carriage within County Roscommon of 6½d per ton per mile, and with nowhere in the county more than 40 miles from either Sligo or Galway, the maximum cost of transport to one of those ports would be 21s 8d per ton. With freights on the Royal Canal from Dublin at 14s per ton (though Weld thought that lower rates might be negotiated), the difference of 7s 8d per ton would, at 6½d per ton per mile, cover only 13½ miles of land transport from Richmond Harbour into County Roscommon. Anywhere further than that from Richmond Harbour would save by trading with Sligo or Galway instead.

But even when using the Royal Canal was cheaper, traders might pay more to have their goods delivered to their doors 'almost to a given hour' and to avoid having them left exposed to the weather while awaiting transhipment from canal boat to car or dray.

Finally, even when goods were transported on the Royal to or from towns along the Shannon, the traffic was not always through Richmond Harbour. Weld said that heavy goods from Dublin were sent to Ballymahon on the Royal, then by road the 12 miles to Athlone. That avoided a 12-mile journey by canal to the Shannon followed by a 22-mile journey down the Shannon, including the 'uncertain passage' of Lough Ree: a total of 34 Irish miles, 43¼ 'English'. Rhodes noted the same phenomenon:

At present they are obliged to ship and unship the different species of goods to and from the latter place [Athlone], viz corn, flour, meal, cattle, pigs, &c at Ballymahon, and conveyed a distance of 12 miles overland, which must be tedious and expensive.[27]

The New Royal Canal Company itself sought to attract traffic to its intermediate stations: in an advertisement in 1850 it pointed out that Killashee, on the canal, was only five miles from Lanesborough.[28] Eggs were loaded at Killashee (a crate held

10,800 eggs), having come by road from Lanesborough; at the time Irish egg exports to England were worth £500 a day.[29]

Royal Canal traffic, 1829–31

WELD took the trouble to ask the Royal and Grand canal companies for information about their traffic to and from the Shannon; he got more details from the former than from the latter.

In the three years 1829–31, 173 boats from the Shannon upstream of Tarmonbarry entered the Royal Canal; they carried a total of 4,813.9 tons, an average of about 57 boats and 1,605 tons a year.

In the same period 254 boats from the Shannon downstream of Tarmonbarry (which would include those carrying grain shipped at Lanesborough and any traffic from Lough Ree and Athlone) entered the canal, carrying a total of 8,734 tons, an average of about 85 boats and 2,911 tons a year.

And, again in the same period, 342 boats carried 3,886.75 tons the other way, from the canal to the Shannon: an average of 114 boats a year carrying about 1,295 tons.

The Grand Canal Company provided figures for only one year; its year-end was 30 June rather than 31 December; it did not state the numbers of boats and its classification means that one interesting stream of traffic was not included (TABLE 4).

There was no traffic in either direction between Ballinasloe and Limerick; 453½ tons were 'conveyed up and down between places on the Shannon, below

TABLE 4 : **Traffic between Shannon and Grand Canal at Shannon Harbour: y/e 31 June 1831**

	tons
Athlone to Canal	1,187½
Canal to Athlone	1,203
Ballinasloe to Canal	2,510
Canal to Ballinasloe	3,666½

TABLE 5 : **Traffic between canals and Shannon 1831 and earlier**

Traffic between Royal Canal and Shannon: average for 1829–1831	**Boats**	**tons**
Shannon to Royal Canal	142	4,516
Royal Canal to Shannon	114	1,295
Total	256	5,811
Traffic between Grand Canal and Athlone: and Ballinasloe, 1831	**Boats**	**tons** [30]
Athlone and Ballinasloe to Grand Canal	n/a	3,680
Grand Canal to Athlone and Ballinasloe	n/a	4,870
Total	n/a	8,550

TABLE 6 : **Royal Canal traffic 1836–8**

Item	Toll	1836	1837	1838	From	To
Live pigs (number)	—	36,002	34,349	15,669	between Mullingar and Richmond Harbour	Dublin
Casks of butter (no.)	1¼d	7,639	3,638	3,812	—	—
Corn, meal and potatoes	1¼d	31,746	26,024	15,881	Corn from west of Mullingar including the Shannon; potatoes Cos Longford, Mayo, Sligo, Roscommon	—
Merchandise	1¼d	7,355	6,247	3,373	Dublin	Mostly within 30 miles
Coal and manure	1d	14,344	14,559	4,145	Dublin	Along the line
Turf	1½d	22,992	21,724	10,214	24–59 miles from Dublin	Dublin
Stones, sand, flags, bricks	1–1½d	11,894	16,127	6,414	—	—
Total tonnage		88,334	84,683	40,029		
Total tolls (rounded)		13,095	10,965	6,955		

Compiled from two returns in Appendix B No 6 of the Second Report of the Railway Commissioners

Shannon Harbour, but above Limerick'. This set of figures omits traffic from Limerick and Lough Derg that was conveyed to Shannon Harbour. As that traffic did not serve Roscommon, it did not concern Weld, but it was the realm of the steamers and it would have been interesting to compare it with the non-steamer traffic between Roscommon and the Grand Canal (TABLE 5).

Royal Canal traffic, 1836–8

WELD's description of the canal trade – 'consists principally in corn and butter for exportation, and in heavy and bulky articles from Dublin in return' – does not quite match what the Royal Canal Company told the Railway Commissioners a few years later. It gave figures for 2½ years, ending on 31 March 1838 (TABLE 6). The report does not say which was the half year, but it presumed to be 1838.

Tolls are 'Average Toll per Ton per Mile' but there were upper limits: the maximum toll was 7s 6d per ton for any distance for corn, butter, eggs, meal and flour; 7s for merchandise; 2s 6d for potatoes; 1s 5d for coal; 10d for bricks; 20s per boatload of stone; 15s per boatload of manure. Other special rates were available including a reduced toll on meal and flour carried more than 12 miles to the canal.

A dash indicates that the report did not give information.

Irish food exports and the canals

THE first three items (probably excluding potatoes) include those *en route* to Dublin for export, mostly to Britain. The Acts of Union of 1800, which united the kingdoms of Ireland and Great Britain from 1 January 1801, created a customs union between Britain and Ireland – with the unfortunate side-effect that, except for grain, no official figures were kept for trade between the two kingdoms. Nonetheless, the

TABLE 7 : **Irish exports 1825 and 1835**

Type	Item	Unit	1825	1835
Animal	Cows and oxen	Number	63,524	98,150
	Sheep	Number	72,191	125,452
	Swine	Number	65,919	376,191
Vegetable	Wheat	Quarters	283,340	420,522
	Barley	Quarters	154,822	168,946
	Oats	Quarters	1,503,204	1,575,984
Processed	Meal and flour	Cwt	599,124	1,984,480
	Butter	Cwt	474,161	872,009
	Bacon, hams, beef etc	Cwt	966,531	749,283
	Beer	Gallons	—	2,686,688
Non-food	Linen	Yards	55,114,515	70,365,572

From Part I of the Second Report of the Railway Commissioners

Railway Commissioners were able to compile a set of figures to show the growth in Irish exports between 1825 and 1835 (TABLE 7).

Brinley Thomas estimated that in 1834–6, British imports of grains, meat and butter from Ireland amounted to 9.4% of the output of British agriculture, forestry and fishery;[31] and concluded that imports, mainly from Ireland, supplied about one sixth of the 'grains, butter, meat and livestock available to the British population' in the 1830s and early 1840s.[32] Dublin was Ireland's main port, with combined exports and imports matching those of Cork and Belfast combined,[33] and the availability of steamers facilitated the growth of the livestock trade – Peter Solar estimated that Dublin prices for beef rose by about 20%, compared with Liverpool prices, between 1826 and 1832.[34]

The Shannon steamers, which hauled trade boats to Shannon Harbour and the Grand Canal, existed to provide cargoes for the Dublin to Liverpool steamers of the City of Dublin Steam Packet Company. Livestock needed fast transport: all livestock lost condition when being walked to ports, but pigs in particular lost value. Thomas Rhodes said:

In the great article of fat cattle, sheep, pigs, &c, which are extensively supplied for the English markets, driving them to Dublin, in many instances upwards of 100 miles, is found to deteriorate them very much in value; besides the expense and risk on the road, which in their present state must be something considerable, a great saving would be effected in these matters, as well as in all other produce.[35]

Sweeter, less heavily-salted butter also benefited from fast transport. The City of Dublin Steam Packet Company's Irish Sea steamer **Ballinasloe**, built in 1829, was the first purpose-built cattle carrier, with forced ventilation to the cattle holds; another steamer had a dedicated 'cool chamber' for butter.[36]

In 1835 the Shannon steamers hauled 20,000 tons from the Shannon; between 1822 and 1837 the amount of traffic from the Shannon to the Grand Canal rose from

3,121 to 20,534 tons, most of the increase being in exportable food and byproducts. The tonnage carried on the canal rose by 60%, from 134,939 to 215,910 tons, and the toll income by 50% in the same period;[37] tonnage continued to rise to 239,014 tons in 1844 and 264,127 in 1847.[38]

In contrast, the Royal Canal's total tonnage in 1845 was more or less the same (88,142 tons) as it had been in the mid-1830s.[39] The question is why its performance did not improve over that period; I do not know the answer. The road network in County Roscommon could have compensated for the deficiencies of the Shannon: it could have carried livestock and produce to Richmond Harbour as easily as it did to Sligo or Galway.

It may be – and I admit that this is speculation – that the counties around the western end of the Royal Canal produced relatively little that needed fast transport to Dublin and across the Irish Sea. Grain could be carried by 'long sea' from Sligo or Galway, with the length of the voyage being largely irrelevant. Pigs and eggs, by contrast, could benefit from fast transport and did form part of the Royal traffic, but it did not have the volume of livestock traffic that the Grand carried.

The Royal Canal and the Shannon Commissioners

THE exertions of the Shannon Commissioners, who spent almost £600,000 throughout the 1840s improving the navigation of the river Shannon, do not seem to have been sufficient to improve trade from the Shannon to the Royal Canal (TABLE 8).[40]

The figures need qualification. The later years of the period saw the start of the Great Famine, which the Commissioners referred to as 'the general depression of trade in this country, consequent on the severe pressure of the last few years'.[42] Furthermore, the Shannon works themselves caused increases in Shannon traffic in some cases but disruption in others; much of the work on the upper Shannon was in the later years. The Grand Canal figure for 1849 was reduced because a breach closed the canal for nine months.[43]

TABLE 8 : **Traffic between canals and Shannon in the 1840s**

tons (rounded)	from canals to Shannon			from Shannon to canals		
Year	Grand	Royal	Total	Grand	Royal	Total
1840	12,878	1,389	14,367	14,548	1,919	16,721 [41]
1841	13,251	1,741	14,992	15,329	1,925	17,254
1842	12,824	1,362	14,186	13,354	3,118	16,472
1843	11,173	1,306	12,479	13,532	2,684	16,216
1844	9,446	1,478	10,924	13,863	975	14,838
1845	11,687	1,290	12,977	17,286	1,275	18,561
1846	15,353	218	15,571	13,582	251	13,833
1847	26,106	37	26,143	15,499	120	15,619
1848	17,572	432	18,004	12,086	137	12,223
1849	9,352	2,320	11,672	14,370	713	15,083

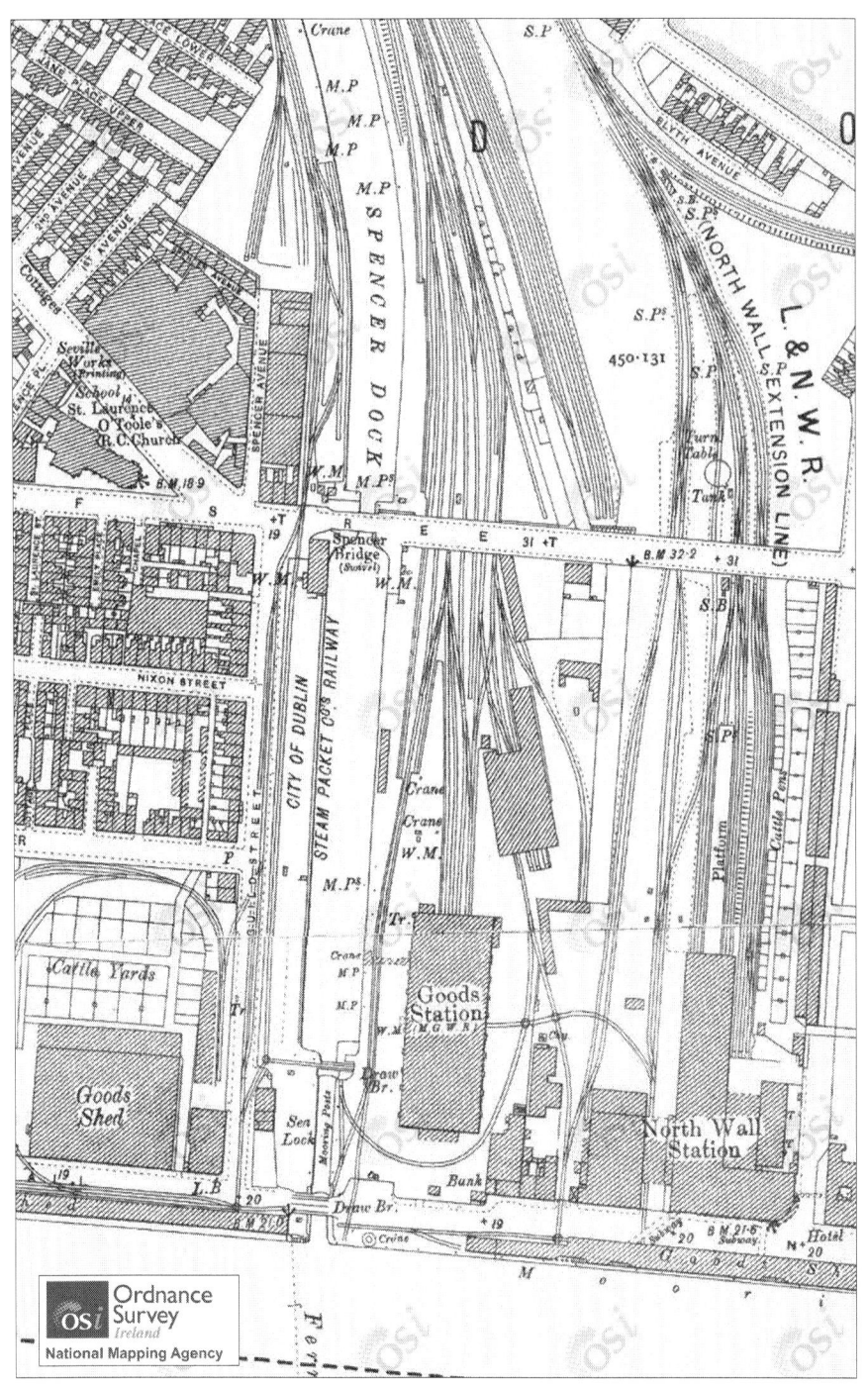

Railway and canal at the river Liffey in Dublin, c.1910
Ordnance Survey Ireland

The Famine and the river works reduced traffic in the short term but the canal's long-term decline was caused by two people: Sir John Macneill and Sir Robert Peel. Macneill, an engineer, reported on the possibility of a railway from Dublin to Mullingar and Athlone and persuaded investors that it should be built along the route of the Royal Canal, which the Midland Great Western Railway [MGWR] proceeded to do.[44] Peel, UK Prime Minister in 1846, repealed the Corn Laws, against the protests of landowners who benefited from high prices.

As wheat from outside the United Kingdom became available at lower cost, the share of tillage (including grain production) in total Irish agricultural output fell from 65% in 1850–4 to 21% in 1904–13.[45] Between 1850 and 1874 the five-year annual average exports of Irish live cattle, sheep and pigs to Great Britain trebled.[46] Isaac Weld had seen the potential:

The facility with which the transport is now effected, has induced some of the more adventurous graziers in Ireland, to send their cattle to England, on their own account, thus pocketing the gains which used to be divided between the cattle jobbers and the Dublin salesmen.[47]

However, he was wrong about the mode of transport to the ports:

Cattle boats are already established between Ballinasloe and Dublin, by which fatted animals can be conveyed along the Grand Canal, in a given time, and with the least possible liability to accident; and no doubt, similar establishments will sooner or later be made at Tarmonbarry, for the transportation of cattle by the Royal Canal, from the northern parts of the county. Improvements of this nature are still in their infancy, and the country as yet scarcely knows its own resources.

Some cattle boats operated on the Royal, but a much more important carrier arrived in 1848 when the Midland Great Western Railway reached Mullingar:

The Company having made Arrangements for the Daily Conveyance of Light Goods and Cattle, they will be taken down by the Three o'Clock Train from Dublin, and brought up by the Ten o'Clock Train from Mullingar … Goods and Cattle must be at the different Stations an hour before the starting of the Trains … A Special Cattle Train will leave Mullingar on Wednesdays at Twelve o'Clock, noon.[48]

The line reached Athlone, Ballinasloe and Galway in 1851; Longford in 1855; Boyle and Sligo in 1862; Westport in 1866. The Midland, with its own dock on the Liffey and excellent connections to Dublin port, became, as its Manager Joseph Tatlow called it, 'the principal cattle-carrying line in Ireland'.[49]

The Royal Canal's choice of line was at last vindicated but its technology was outdated. The railway could carry more cattle at higher speeds than could any canal boat; high-earning trade was no longer available to the canal. It could be said that, in its early years, the Royal Canal failed because of the excellence of the roads and, in its later years, because of the superiority of the railway.

THREE

Some Royal Canal carriers

In January 1846, after the Midland Great Western Railway [MGWR] had taken over, it reduced the Royal Canal tolls on corn, meal, flour, potatoes, butter, bran, rapeseed, bacon, beef, pork and 'other articles of general merchandize'. Between Dublin and Hill of Down, 36 miles away, the tolls were set at one penny per mile. Westward of Hill of Down the rate was less than 1d per mile; for the 90 miles to either Longford or Richmond Harbour, the toll was only 5s 10d (70 pence) for 90 miles.

The new rates were to apply from 2 February 1846. At the same time, the 'principal Boat Owners' agreed to reduce freights and a scale of charges per ton was agreed. It ranged from 1s 10d (22 pence) for the 11 miles from Dublin to the Rye Aqueduct to 11s 8d (140 pence) for 90 miles to Richmond Harbour or Longford.

The general regulations, which comprise several other reductions to Boat Owners and Carriers on the Canal, may be had at the Company's different Offices and Stations … The rates and regulations for parcels by the Company's Packet Boats have also undergone considerable reductions and improvements in despatch and delivery.[50]

Parcels

The Dublin section of Slater's 1846 *Directory* has lists of conveyances (passenger-carrying coaches, railways, omnibuses, cars and caravans) and of carriers.[51] Carriers were listed 'with their [Dublin] warehouses, wharfs and inns' and then again by the towns they served, annotated to show whether they carried by rail, road or canal. The list showed only two Dublin-based carriers on the Royal Canal:

— the Royal Canal Company (Samuel Draper, Secretary)
  at Broadstone in Dublin
— John M'Cann & Sons, Liffey lock, North Wall, where the
  Royal Canal joins the River Liffey.

I believe that the Royal Canal Company's inclusion as a carrier reflects the fact that its passenger boats also carried small packages or parcels. The company's officers included:

Mr H.N. Webb, Collector at Mullingar, and Parcel Officer;

Mr Hugh O'Neill, Collector at Longford, and Parcel Officer.

Mr James Neary at Richmond Harbour was merely a Collector: the passage boats did not serve Richmond Harbour so no parcels were collected or delivered there.[52] I have found no evidence to suggest that the Royal Canal Company or the Midland Great Western Railway carried goods on their own canal at this time.[53]

The Royal Canal Company offered to serve these destinations:

Athlone, Ballinafad, Ballymahon, Balnacarig, Balnalack, Boyle, Boyne aqueduct, Carrick on Shannon, Castlerea, Colooney, Coolnahay, Downs Bridge, Dromod, Drumsna, Ferns, Glasson, Hill of Down, Junction [which may be the junction between the main line and the Longford Branch], Kenagh, Kilcock, Lanesborough, Leixlip, Longford, Maynooth, Moyvalley, Mullingar, Newcastle, Newtownforbes, Rathowen, Roscommon, Ruskey, Rye aqueduct, Sligo, Terlicken, Thomastown, Toome Bridge.

Many of those places are not along the canal, so the connecting road services for passengers presumably carried parcels too.

McCann

In October 1839, Matthew Walsh of Glen-House, Sligo, placed an advert in *The Freeman's Journal*:

LISSADILL OYSTERS

Having made a contract with Mr Daniel O'Hara, of No 1, French-street, for the entire and exclusive Sale of all my Oysters, known by the name of Cullamore and Lissadill, and having made arrangement with Mr M'Cann, owner of the Fly Boats, for the speedy transmission of the Oysters from hence to Dublin, no disappointment can take place. The first barge arrives THIS DAY, and sent per Order Twice a Week.

As to the quality, flavour, and size, these Oysters cannot be surpassed, and one trial will prove the excellence of them.

M W having taken unusual care of these Oysters, he recommends them as far superior to any that has hitherto been sent to Dublin.[54]

Mr O'Hara added a few words about his own establishment, where he offered 'that delicious dish, so much admired, Cow-heel and Tripe', as well as Beef Steak and Oyster Sauce and 'All Malt Liquors of the best description'.

Mr M'Cann [McCann] was not quoted in the ad, but the Sligo oysters are an interesting example of a perishable cargo that needed speedy delivery across the width of Ireland. According to Isaac Slater's *Directory* for 1846, his boats served

Arvagh, Athlone, Ballaghaderin, Ballina, Ballinamore, Ballyfarnon, Ballymahon, Ballymore, Ballymote, Boyle, Carrick on Shannon, Castlerea, Dromod, Drumkerrin [Drumkeeran?], Drumlish, Drumshambo, Drumsna, Dunmore, Edgeworthstown, Elphin, Fenagh, Granard, Lanesborough, Longford, Mohill, Roscommon, Ruskey, Strokestown, Tenelick Mills, Tulsk.

He too offered a wide range of destinations beyond the canal, presumably linked by cars on the roads, into Counties Longford, Cavan, Roscommon, Westmeath, Mayo and Sligo.

Some years earlier, in 1838, McCann seems to have had three boats (although Peter Clarke shows him as having five).[55] His was no means the largest fleet, yet McCann seems to have been an influential trader – if only because his influence was denied.[56] At a meeting of Royal and Grand Canal traders in February 1853 John Ennis, Chairman of the MGWR, denied that the 1846 reduction in tolls was 'the result of a private bargain or arrangement with a very influential gentleman then trading upon the Royal Canal ... The reduction ... was not the result of a private arrangement with Mr M'Cann, or any other individual'.[57]

McCann was the only Royal Canal trader quoted in the Second Report of the Railway Commissioners in 1838, which gave an extract from a letter addressed to the Secretary of the Royal Canal Company, by Messrs M'Cann & Sons:

We beg to observe, that from the great accommodation afforded by the City of Dublin Steam Company, we are enabled to discharge our three boats (which, from the combination against us, are obliged to travel together) in one day ... The Trade Boats travel at the rate of about 16 to 20 English miles in one day, including delays.[58]

The CoDSPCo

McCann mentioned the City of Dublin Steam Packet Company [CODSPCO]. That company's adverts throughout the 1830s listed its Irish Sea and Shannon steamers, adding:

In addition to the above, the Company have 52 Trade Boats (24 built of timber, and 28 of iron), averaging 50 tons burden, for the carriage of Goods, Produce, and Live Stock, by the Grand and Royal Canals, and the River Shannon, between Dublin and the Interior.[59]

Clarke does not include the City of Dublin Steam Packet Company, or the Inland Steam Navigation Company which it subsumed, in his list of boat owners.[60] Delany says that Charles Wye Williams, principal of the steam company, had 'a number of horse-drawn trade-boats on the Royal Canal' used to carry coal slack to, and his patented fuel from, his peat manufactory at Cappagh Bog on the Royal Canal.[61]

The extent of the company's advertising, however, suggests a much larger scale of operations than that, although according to the Railway Commissioners' Second Report the company had agents along the line of the Grand but not of the Royal

Canal.[62] On the other hand, the report quoted the Secretary to the Royal Canal Company as saying

and concerning the Trade Boats, there are some on the Navigation that have been built upon a new principle; those are employed, conveying cattle, by the Inland Steam Company, and it is hoped that the Merchant Traders will avail themselves of the improvement effected in the construction of boats.[63]

The 'new principle' was not described but it is possible that the reference was to the iron cattle boats described by Mary John Knott in 1836:

Commodious iron boats have been provided by the [steam] company, for conveying cattle, sheep, and pigs, to Dublin, from whence they can be transmitted daily to the Liverpool market. Those boats are built high above the water, with a door-way in the side, through which the cattle are driven in and fastened in rows along the hold: the smaller animals are secured on deck by railing placed around.[64]

In 1851, at the MGWR's half-yearly meeting, it was reported that the directors had

recently made arrangements with the City of Dublin Steam Packet Company for the extension of their inland establishment to the Upper Shannon, in connexion with your railway, and the transfer of their trade-boats to the Royal Canal.[65]

However, more research is required into the extent of the company's operations on the Royal Canal.

The MGWR as a carrier

ACCORDING to Ruth Delany, the MGWR decided in 1871 to act as carriers on their own canal;[66] Peter Clarke gives the date as 1870.[67] It seems, though, that the MGWR tried carrying twice: in the 1870s using steam (see Chapter 6) and in the 1850s using horses.

On 24 June 1852 a general extraordinary meeting of the shareholders of the MGWR was held at Broadstone to consider whether, under the Canal Carriers Act 1845,[68] the company should exercise the power to become carriers on the Royal Canal.[69]

The meeting's Chairman, James Stirling, said that they 'were not exceedingly anxious to take upon them the duties of carriers' but that they wanted to be prepared in case of emergency so that they would not lose any possible benefits. They did not intend to compete with the existing carriers but

If it became necessary it was their intention to place tugging power on the Shannon, which would be hired out to any other traders upon the canal that would continue to send their boats up and down the Shannon.

In response to a question from Mr Pilsworth, the Chairman said that the company

The MGWR Broadstone building
Author

did not intend to 'make any difference between their own boats and those of the regular traders'. A resolution authorising the company to become carriers was then carried.

Just over a year later, in August 1853, the company sought tenders from hauliers for 'the Haulage of their Trade Boats to and from Dublin and Longford and the River Shannon'; tenders could be submitted for some or all of the work but security was required.[70] One John Wallis won some or all of the work but he did not last long: in November 1853 an auctioneer said that Wallis had surrendered his contract and was therefore selling

Thirty First-class Draught and Harness Horses, chiefly sound, young, and powerful, all purchased within the last Eighteen Months at high figures, and now in the best heart and corn-fed condition.[71]

The contract seems to have been for only one year at a time because tenders were sought again in October 1854 for haulage 'from and after the 14th November next'. The company had great hopes for the canal; at the half-yearly meeting on 22 September 1854 Mr Cowper, chairman of the Canal Committee, said that, although the canal had lost £700 in the previous year,

it was improving every day – in fact, it was a property they were getting in love with more and more every day, and next half year they would be in a far different position with respect to it from what they were now.[72]

An 1857 advert shows that the boats did not serve anywhere east of Mullingar, where they might compete with the railway; nor did they serve Longford, which the railway had reached in 1855.

26

The Company's Trade Boats ply daily to the following stations on the Canal and river Shannon, viz: – Mullingar, Balnacarrig, Ballymahon, Richmond Harbour, Roosky, Carrick-on-Shannon, and Lanesborough, at each of which places the Company have agents.[73]

The boats served three stations on the river Shannon; I do not know whether steam 'tugging power' was used and, if it was, who provided it.

By March 1861, the directors were reporting falling profits from the canal. At the half-yearly meeting on 21 March 1861, they said:

there is a diminution of profits as compared with the last half year of £1,300. The total receipts for this half year are £5,583 as against £6,858 for the corresponding period of the previous year.[74]

The MGWR line from Athlone to Westport had reached the town of Roscommon in 1860; the directors thought that had reduced water-borne traffic from Lanesborough, while severe frost had 'locked up' the canal in December 1860. But six months later the Royal Canal income had fallen again, for a different set of reasons.

The income from the Royal Canal during the previous half year was £7,612; this half year, I am sorry to say, it has fallen to £6,018, showing a deficiency of £1,600.[75] *To account for that it is only necessary for me to refer to the general state of the country in the carrying department, farming produce and goods of that description.*[76]

There had also been an incursion by the Grand Canal Company on to the upper Shannon, but a compromise agreement had removed that threat. However, the MGWR gave up carrying on 31 January 1863 and the boats and 'other plant' were sold.[77] At the half-yearly meeting on 19 March 1863 the Chairman said that

they had found it necessary to surrender the navigation of the canal to private enterprise; and he believed the company, and the Canal Committee particularly, had arrived at a wise conclusion on that subject.[78]

At the half-yearly meeting on 17 September 1863, the Chairman stated:

We do not mean to say that the canal has not its proper description of traffic – corn and lumber should at all times go by the canal; but I am at liberty to say, and I do say with great satisfaction, that though we are not receiving as much gross money as we formerly did while carriers on the canal, the nett balance to the credit of the company upon the mere tollage is considerably in excess. Therefore, I say, it was wise in the directors to disconnect themselves as carriers with the Royal Canal, and to leave it with the public to be their own carriers.[79]

Other carriers

SLATER'S 1846 *Directory* lists six corn merchants in Longford, all with addresses at Market Square.[80] One, John Delany, also had an address in Sligo and presumably exported via that port, carrying by road; the other five all had Dublin as well as Longford addresses. John McCann was listed too: he was the only one listed as a Dublin-based carrier, but three of the other four firms also carried goods regularly towards Dublin: Francis & John Pilsworth's boats left Longford on Mondays and Thursdays, as did Thomas & Edward Duffy's boats; Farrelly & Killard's boats left once a week. Only Nicholas Butler did not offer transport. The Duffy and Pilsworth boats also carried goods in both directions from Mullingar. My guess is that carrying goods from others helped these merchants to cover the costs of their own fleets.

Clarke lists these other large traders (with their numbers of boats): Duffy Bros (12), Pilsworth (9), Dunne (8), Kelly (6), Murtagh (6). Smaller traders had only one, two, three or four boats.[81]

Horses on board

In his address at the MGWR half-yearly meeting on 7 September 1876, the Chairman Sir Ralph Cusack said that the largest trader on the Royal Canal was about to retire from business because of ill health.[82] As a result, Sir Ralph said that the MGWR intended to begin carrying on the canal to avoid inconvenience to those who sent by canal 'materials that are not exactly suited for a railway' (see Chapter 6).[83]

It seems likely that the trader he had in mind was Nicholas Butler because, on 11 September 1876, the *Freeman's Journal* carried an ad from Michael Crooke, a Dublin auctioneer, who said that he had been

favoured with instruction from Nicholas Butler, Esq, who has retired from the Royal Canal carrying trade, to sell by public auction [Mr Butler's equipment].[84]

The list of equipment was a lengthy one including a patent Avery weighing machine, ouncels, beams with chains and bohorns, scales, weights, five winnowing machines, sieves, corn or sack trucks, four little-used 'very superior spring corn drays', floats, harness, scrap iron, a corn bin, office furniture, barrels, cases, crates, hampers, bottles, jars, tins, timber, a grinding stone, a pair of panelled doors and some corn ladders.

The main attraction, though, was Mr Butler's fleet of boats:

His four superior well-known canal boats, built to order by Barrington, Ringsend, and lately trading between Dublin and Longford and Mullingar &c. Viz: – No 113, No 114, No 115, No 116. All iron built, of the very best materials, and carrying over fifty tons each, on a very light draught of water, lately thoroughly overhauled and refitted at very considerable expense, with stabling on board each boat for two horses, men's cabin with bunks, caboose, &c … Also, the planking, poles, boat covers, nearly new; and four double sets harness and tackling.[85]

I cannot recall seeing any other evidence that horses towing Irish canal-boats were stabled on board the boats and I cannot imagine why the practice was adopted.

FOUR

Romance brought up the nine-fifteen*

Or
The whore who held the mortgage on the Royal

At the first half-yearly meeting of the Midland Great Western Railway Company [MGWR], held at 23 College Green, Dublin on 21 August 1845, James Maley, the company's solicitor, read the directors' report, which explained why and how the company had bought the Royal Canal.

The proprietors are generally aware, that under the agreement entered into for the purchase of the Royal Canal, which has been confirmed by your act of incorporation, this company is entitled to immediate possession of the canal property, on payment of the first instalment of the purchase-money, within one month after the passing of the act. – Notice has already been given to the Canal Company, that your board is prepared to pay this sum, amounting to £60,000, and to perform all the requisites necessary upon their part, to entitle them to take possession of the Canal and its appendages, in accordance with the terms of their agreement; but the 29th of September being the termination of the current half year of the Canal Company, it has been mutually agreed that this company shall take up possession of the canal immediately after. The advantages of this purchase may not be sufficiently understood, and your board therefore deem it desirable to state the following particulars respecting it, viz: –

The amount to be paid by this company for the Royal Canal, and all its appendages, is £298,059/5/2, say in round numbers £300,000

* Kipling (from 'The King')

This sum is to be paid in quarterly instalments of £30,000 each, spread over a period, after the first deposit, of two years, and in return the company obtain: –

A saving on the cost of land and works on the first fifty miles out of Dublin (comprising two most valuable positions for stations in Dublin) say £3,500 per mile – £175,000 … Income for water, and other rents, upwards of £2,700 per ann, say £50,000

Total £225,000. Leaving the cost of the whole water-way and works of nearly 100 miles of canal navigation, the construction of which cost about one and a half million sterling, for the sum of about seventy-five thousand pounds sterling.

For some years past, the nett revenues of the canal have been equal to an average return of about £15,000 per annum. The improvements now in progress on the Upper Shannon, and other districts connected with the navigation, must open large and productive sources of additional traffic.

The transfer of the canal will also give us possession of nearly all the land necessary for the construction of the line of railway to Mullingar, and enable us to proceed with the immediate construction of the works, for which the necessary preparations are already in progress. It must, therefore, be manifested to the proprietors, that the purchase is eminently advantageous to the interests of your company.[86]

At the next meeting, the directors' report pointed out a further advantage: that, as well as providing an income, the canal afforded an opportunity for 'the cheap construction of the railway'.[87]

The Royal Canal directors became 'trustees for the proprietors or stockholders of the said canal to receive the purchase money for the said canal'.[88] In October 1849, the MGWR began to draw down a government loan of £500,000 to enable it to extend its line to Galway on the west coast of Ireland. The loan documents showed that the sum of £135,860/15/8 of the purchase money for the canal was still outstanding.[89]

Within a year, however, the Royal Canal trustees had been paid off. At the half-yearly meeting held on 27 September 1850, Henry Beausire, Secretary, reported that

The directors have the pleasure to state that the mortgage for the balance due of the purchase of the canal has been transferred on advantageous terms, and the amount paid in full to the trustees of the late canal company.[90]

The company had found a new lender who had enabled them to pay off the trustees. But although the lender changed, the loan itself continued in being: it was still on the books in 1877. At the company's half-yearly meeting on 1 March of that year the Chairman said:

In the last half year we have paid off, as we had powers to do, £10,000 of the canal loan, which was a loan out at 4¼ per cent for £135,800, borrowed by the company from Mrs Kelly and others.[91]

The rate of repayment was restricted but in 1877 the company could borrow at 4 per cent and he hoped to have the loan paid off in seven years; the 'canal loan' was reported to have been paid off by March 1886.[92]

The loan

THE arrival of the new lender had excited much interest in July 1850.

The topic of the week in the money market has been the advance by Mrs Kelly, whose name has been so frequently before the public in the celebrated will case, of the large sum of £135,000 to the Midland Great Western Railway Company, to enable the latter to discharge the balance of the purchase money due to the Royal Canal Company, being about that amount.

Mrs Kelly receives a transfer of the canal direct from the Canal Company, and becomes the first incumbrancer on it, the total cost having been upwards of £400,000. She has, of course, the security of the Railway Company in addition, and as far as Mrs Kelly is concerned, the security may be considered undoubted. The transaction is, however, an advantageous one for the company, as they have agreed to pay Mrs Kelly 5 per cent, while they paid 6 per cent to the Canal Company; there is therefore a diminution of £1,350 per annum in the interest paid by the company.[93]

According to MeasuringWorth.com, the purchasing power of £135,000 in 1850 is that of £12.6 million in 2013.[94] Mrs Kelly was a wealthy woman; her wealth was the result of her own efforts throughout a life that might have provided material for a dozen Victorian novelists. As the *Daily News* of London put it in 1856:

There is hardly to be found, perhaps, in the voluminous varieties of French romance, a story more full of strange and startling vicissitudes than that which the life of Sarah Kelly might supply.[95]

Over a period of about sixty years, Sarah Kelly and her life featured in many court cases and in newspaper reports thereon. There were, of course, conflicts in the evidence; there were even more in the reports, which provide accounts that are often partisan, that conflict on points of detail and that in some cases appear to be based on speculation or imagination.[96]

In 1988 Vera Hughes wrote *The Strange Story of Sarah Kelly*, in which she covered not only Sarah Kelly's life but also the lives of her heirs.[97] However, the connection to the MGWR was not included. Furthermore, Sarah Kelly is not mentioned in published histories of the Royal Canal or of the MGWR.[98]

Sarah Kelly's early life

SARAH Birch was born in Ramsgate in Kent in around 1801. In 1807 her father, John Birch, moved to Broadstairs, where he kept an inn. At the age of fifteen Sarah was seduced by a young Irishman, Joshua Paul Meredith, who had an income of £4,000–£5,000 a year. He took her first to London and then to Ireland where, after their son was born, Meredith abandoned Sarah.

In April 1819, at the Court of Common Pleas in Dublin, John Birch sought damages of £5,000 from Meredith for the seduction of his daughter.[99] He was awarded £2,000, and costs of 6d, but it seems that the sum was never paid.

The infant son is no longer mentioned but Sarah herself had to live. Vera Hughes acknowledges that it was suggested that she turned to prostitution but thinks it more likely that Sarah was a mistress, a 'kept woman'. The *Daily News* of 1856 put it this way:

the unhappy woman, whose wrongs had enlisted for the hour the worthless sympathy of the sentimental and the idle, was once more brought face to face with hunger and privation. Who shall tell the struggles and remorseful efforts that she may have made to escape the gulf of shame into which she was eventually drawn! We dare not dwell upon the fearful theme, or give unguarded utterances to questions that suggest themselves to every humane and merciful mind that has calmly contemplated the terrible temptations that beset despair. Suffice it to say, that for a period little short of 20 years this ill-fated woman lived in the condition of an outcast in the city of Dublin, and that at the end of that time she became the mistress, and eventually the wife of a Mr Kelly, who had amassed a very considerable fortune by the profession of the law.[100]

Sarah and Edmund Kelly

EDMUND Kelly was a solicitor and a land-agent. The *Sussex Advertiser* described him thus:

Mr Kelly ... was an Irish attorney of the old school, resembling the attorney mentioned in Phillips's 'Life of Curran', and who was in the habit of feasting embarrassed clients with claret and venison at night, and selling them out of house and land the next day.[101] *He had realised a large real and personal property, amounting to nearly a million in value. He married her though verging on his eighty-fourth year, and the following morning Mrs Kelly persuaded him to make his will, leaving her the entire of his property, to the total exclusion of his relations, even to an illegitimate daughter.*[102]

Edmund and Sarah were certainly living together by 1828. They may have been married in 1827 but, being unable to find the marriage certificate, they went through a second ceremony on 15 April 1838.[103] Edmund's last will was made on 21 April 1838;[104] the couple went to England, where they met Kelly's daughter, now a Mrs

Yeatman, who sued her father for assaulting her.[105] In 1840 Kelly bought an estate, at Ballinderry, near the town of Moate in County Westmeath but he owned several other estates, including one at Uckfield in East Sussex.[106]

The court cases

EDMUND died in February 1845 and was buried in Kensal Green in London. The first challenge to Sarah's inheritance came from Edmund Crofton Kelly, the heir-at-law, who would have been entitled to inherit the real property had Edmund died intestate.[107] The case was suspended after the first day when a jury member became ill so the basis of Edmund Crofton Kelly's case was not shown; he settled a month later for £7,500.[108]

In 1848 another Kelly relative, Elizabeth Thewles (later Mrs Dease), contested the validity of Edmund Kelly's will. Sarah Kelly won in the lower court but, in 1851, the Court of Delegates reversed the decision. In effect, it decided that the will was fraudulent and it awarded all costs against Mrs Kelly.[109] It was during that legal process that Mrs Kelly lent money to the MGWR. She also put £35,000, in Bank of Ireland and MGWR shares, in the hands of her solicitor, George Birch, said to be her nephew.

Sarah Kelly appealed the decision of the Court of Delegates and, on 8 July 1852, the Lord Chancellor said that he would 'advise her Majesty to issue a new commission to review the decision of that Court'.[110] Her Majesty did so.

The important will case of Kelly v Thewles, involving a property of more than £300,000 in the funds, &c, and £3,000 per annum from estates in land, came to a final judgment on Saturday, in a commission of review ... the unanimous decision of the court on Saturday was pronounced in favour of the appellant, thus establishing the will and reversing the decision of the Court of Delegates.[111]

Sarah Kelly had won. Unfortunately she was not finished with the courts. George Birch refused to return her money. She offered a reward for his arrest; he was charged but acquitted; she took a civil case against him. He claimed that the money was a gift and that he was Sarah's son.

Birch was also sued by Mr Morton, now the husband of the former Mrs Yeatman, Edmund Kelly's daughter; Birch was accused of committing an assault with a criminal intent on Mrs Morton. And Elizabeth Thewles (now Dease) petitioned the Lord Chancellor to have Sarah charged with perjury; the Lord Chancellor dismissed the petition.[112]

Within sight of the line

SARAH Kelly's house at Ballinderry, outside Moate in County Westmeath, was within sight of the Midland Great Western Railway line to Athlone. The estate was managed by her nephew George Strevens.

On 8 April 1856 Sarah Kelly, George Strevens and her solicitor and 'intimate personal friend' Christopher Campion went to visit a field whence stones were being picked.[113, 114] Campion, who had previously discovered discrepancies in Strevens's accounts, went back to the house. Two men, wearing veils and women's cloaks, came from a plantation about a mile away and entered the field. Sarah Kelly ran from them, but tripped and fell; each of the men fired a bullet into her head and then left.

Strevens ran back to the house, pursued briefly by the murderers, and summoned Campion, who preceded him to the field. As Strevens arrived, Campion said to a Mr Flood 'This is the man that got it done' and, to Strevens, 'Well, Mr Strevens, how was this job done? Where did they come from, and where did they go to? When you say they did not pursue you any more, you were not the man they wanted to shoot.'

Strevens and four other men were arrested. Strevens was charged 'as a participant in the lamentable murder ... but was subsequently discharged' and proceeded to sue Campion for slander.[115] He won his case – but was awarded only 6*d* [2½p] in damages and 6*d* in costs.[116]

Hughes and others believe that local men carried out the murder to prevent evictions, but they seem to rely largely on later folklore.[117] A tenant-devised plot cannot explain how the murderers knew when and where they would find their victim.

The legatees

STREVENS and Campion, and others, benefited under Sarah's will, but her nephew Robert Preston Bayley was the principal beneficiary. He died at Brighton on 9 April 1876, aged 52.[118] The report of the next half-yearly meeting of the Midland Great Western Railway included this:

The chairman regretted to have to announce the death of one of their directors, Mr Robert Preston Bailey [sic], in room whom of [sic] Viscount Gough, who had always taken the greatest interest in their company, was appointed (hear, hear).[119]

The railway connection had been maintained.

FIVE

Mallet's Insistent Pontoon

The Royal Canal nowadays runs from the river Liffey, in Dublin, to the river Shannon. For most of the nineteenth century, though, it had a second Dublin terminus: at Broadstone, near Phibsboro.

The Broadstone line

In evidence to the Railway Commissioners, whose *Second Report* was published in 1838, the Royal Canal Company Engineer, Mr Tarrant, said that the canal had two branches off the main line. One, near the western end, went to Longford while the other 'branch from the Broadstone level is 2 miles, when it enters the River Liffey'.[120]

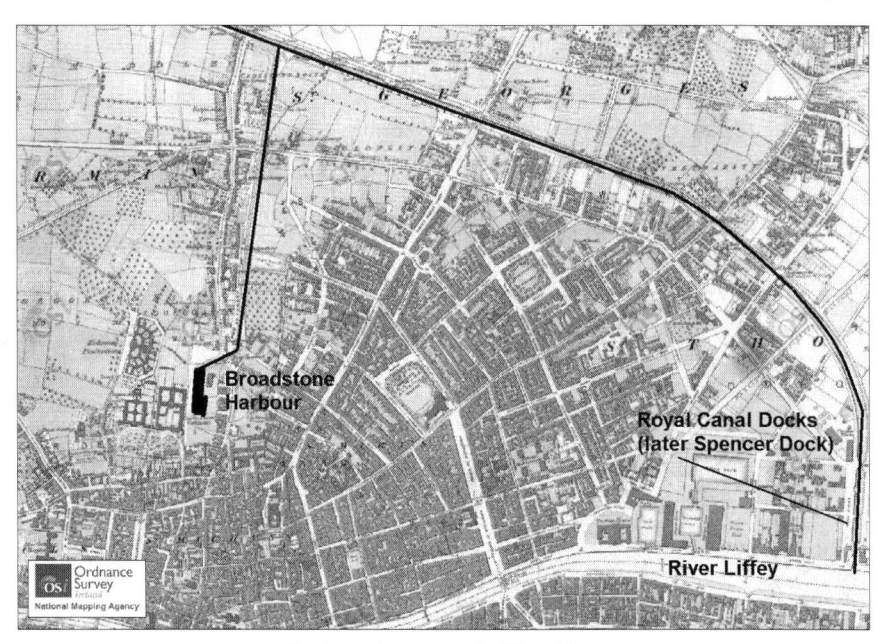

The Broadstone and Liffey Lines
Ordnance Survey Ireland

35

In other words, he saw the Broadstone as the main line; the line to the Liffey was a branch, and thus of less importance.

The junction between the Liffey and Broadstone lines was between the fourth and fifth locks on the Liffey line; the Broadstone line, about three quarters of a mile long, had no locks. It ran almost due south for most of its length but, close to its terminus, it turned south-west to cross the road known as Constitution Hill, on the Foster Aqueduct, to reach the Broadstone Harbour.

The harbour was close to the city markets and to many institutions including the Richmond Penitentiary, the Richmond Lunatic Asylum, the North Dublin Union Workhouse, the Female Penitentiary, the Linen Hall and the Queen's Inns. For a time, there was a Royal Canal Hotel at the harbour and that was where the (passenger-carrying) passage-boats left from. The dry docks were on the Broadstone Line and it fed a basin that supplied water to parts of Dublin city.

The railway terminus

WHEN the Midland Great Western Railway Company [MGWR] bought the Royal Canal, it built its Dublin terminus at Broadstone. The first experimental trips on the line were run in April and May 1847 and the line was opened to Enfield [Innfield]

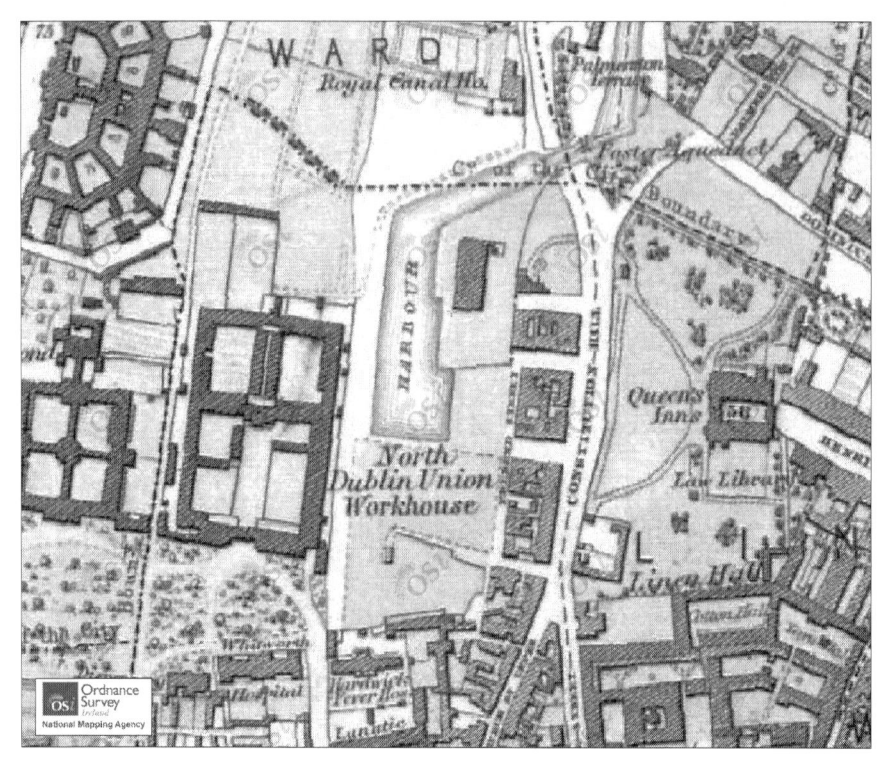

The Broadstone Harbour
Ordnance Survey Ireland

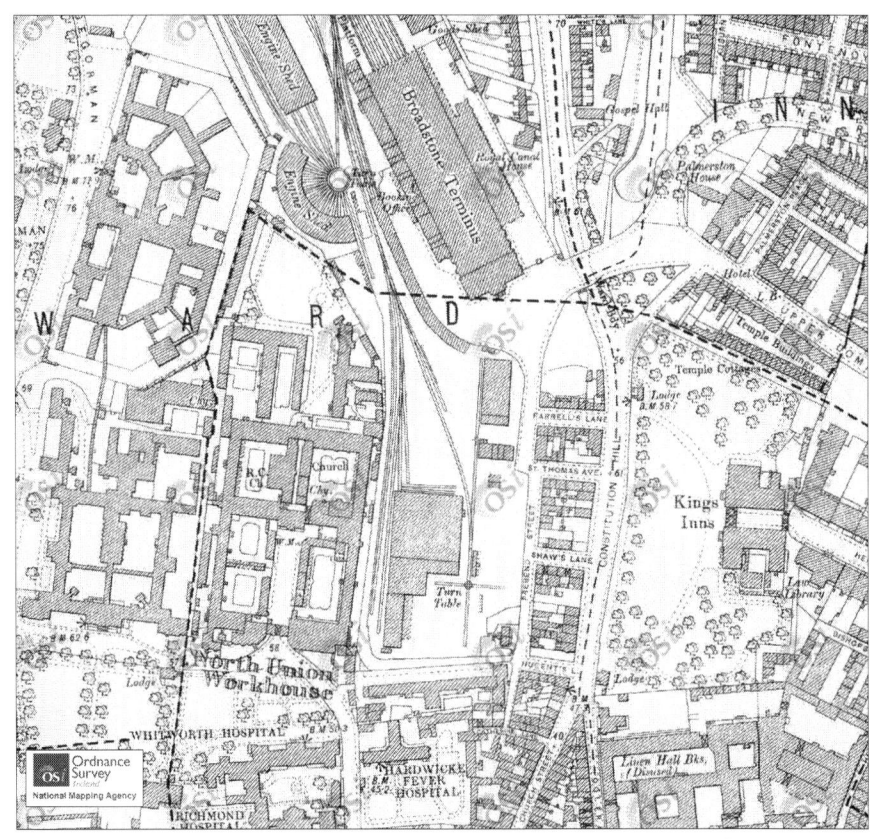

The Broadstone after the harbour was filled in
Ordnance Survey Ireland

on 28 June 1847.[121] The terminus building, designed by John Skipton Mulvany, was opened in 1850; the architectural historian Maurice Craig described it as 'the last building in Dublin to partake of the sublime'.[122]

The railway did not run along the Broadstone line of the canal. It approached Broadstone from the north-west and the terminus was built on that side of the canal harbour. Because the MGWR lines were to run along the canal banks for most of the way to Mullingar, the Broadstone terminus had to be at the same level as the harbour, which was on an embankment 30 feet above the road.

That meant keeping the station buildings north-west of the harbour, but that in turn meant that passengers and vehicles, arriving and departing, would have to cross the canal to get to the station. In 1877, the company did away with that nuisance by filling in the harbour and adapting the Foster Aqueduct to provide access to the station from a new road, later called Western Way. The canal traders were provided with a turning circle and a wharf on the east side of the former aqueduct and they no longer used the Broadstone harbour.

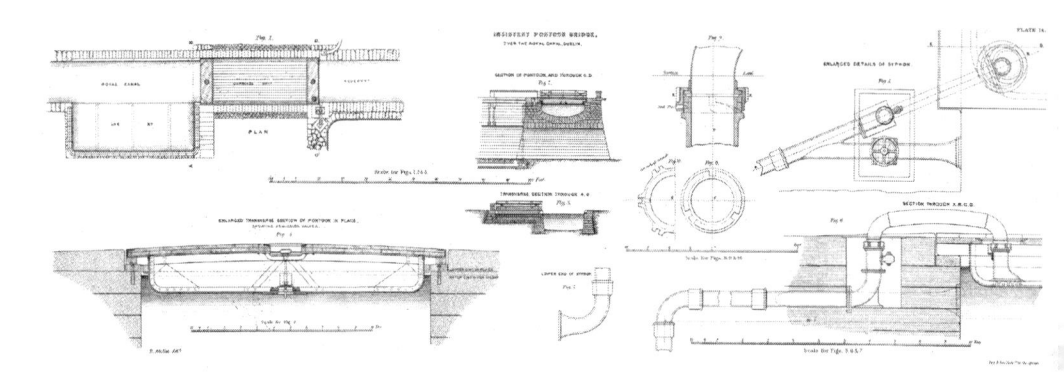

Mallet's Insistent Pontoon
courtesy Institution of Civil Engineers

However, that drastic solution was not considered in 1846. Instead, for thirty years, the MGWR used a pontoon bridge to enable 'vehicles and persons' to cross the canal. The company's engineer-in-chief, G.W Hemans, MInstCE, placed the problem in the hands of Robert Mallet, MInstCE, whose Victoria Foundry premises were close by. On 23 April 1850 Mallet described his solution to the Institution of Civil Engineers; his paper provides details and drawings of what he called an Insistent Pontoon Bridge.[123]

The need for a bridge

THE MGWR was required to maintain 'as free and unimpeded a passage as possible for the traffic on the canal', but it needed to provide for the simultaneous arrival and departure of large numbers of passengers taking or leaving their trains. The company wanted a bridge at least 50 feet wide, but it had to fit into a very small area. The station was close to the canal on one side and the road very close on the other, with not more than 20 feet available for the bridge mechanism.

The canal at the chosen crossing point was 17 feet 4 inches wide and 8 feet deep. Mallet was asked to design a swivel bridge, but he found two problems. First, the surface of the water was only 16 inches below the bank; second, there was not enough space for a 50 foot deck to swivel back into.

At the MGWR's request, he then designed two parallel swivel bridges, each 25 feet wide, and a short distance apart, and got tenders for the construction from his Victoria Foundry. However, he also developed and proposed an alternative design: essentially, to put a deck on a boat and position it between the banks of the canal.

The pontoon

MALLET designed a shallow flat-bottomed iron boat, 50ft 6in. long by 16ft 8in. wide by 2ft 10in. high. It had a timber rubbing-strake along each side.

It carried a deck made of two layers of planking, both caulked and tarred and

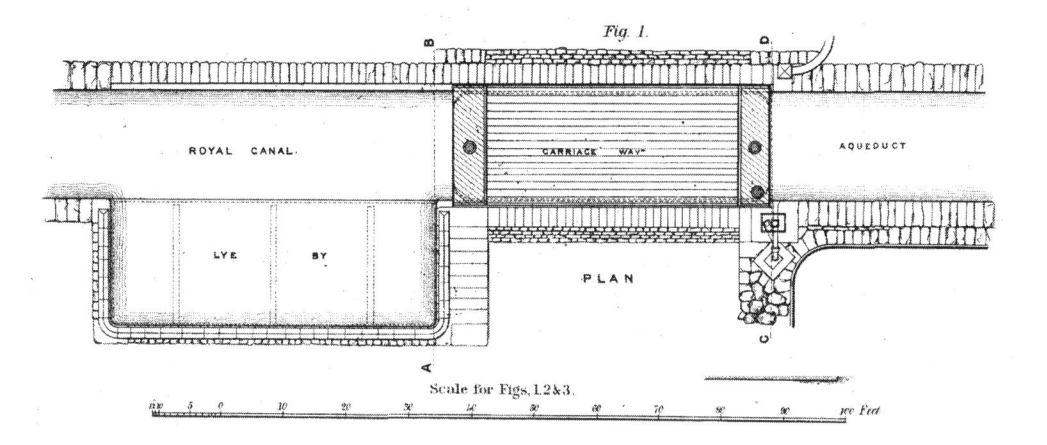

Plan of Mallet's Insistent Pontoon
courtesy Institution of Civil Engineers

the upper layer sanded. There was a wrought-iron handrail at each end, then a five-foot-wide 'footway' for pedestrians; a 'cast-iron wheel-guard of the ordinary form' [a kerb] separated the footways from the carriage-way. The deck was 16 inches wider than the pontoon so that it overlapped the two sides of the canal; it was designed to have a clearance of 2 inches above the sides so that the pontoon could be moved easily.

A shallow 'lye by', just 3 feet deep, was built into which the pontoon was moved when boats needed to pass along the canal; Mallet said that the pontoon could be lifted out from the lye-by on to the bank, using blocks and screw-jacks, for maintenance or painting.

Insistent

MALLET referred to his device as an 'insistent' pontoon bridge, but did not explain what he meant by the term. There are two meanings of 'insistent' that might be relevant. One is unyielding, and Mallet certainly felt that it was undesirable that the pontoon should move under the weight of traffic: 'a floating pontoon would afford a very unstable and inconvenient surface for wheel carriages, &C., to traverse'.[124]

The other sense is from ornithology: '(of a bird's hind-toe) touching the ground with the tip only'.[125]

Mallet's pontoon bridge was designed to float with the deck 2 inches above the sides of the canal, but he wanted it to be fixed in position when in use. Its position was marked by shallow rabbates [rabbets or rebates] in the two sides of the canal; they made the deck level with the banks. And Mallet designed a way of taking on water ballast: its weight would hold the pontoon in position but it could be pumped out again when the pontoon had to be moved to its lye by.

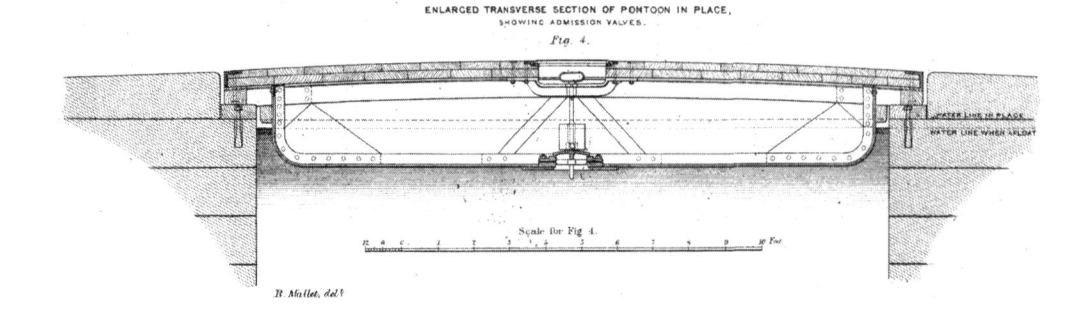

Transverse section of Mallet's Insistent Pontoon
courtesy Institution of Civil Engineers

For taking on water ballast, Mallet put a large valve at each end in the bottom of the pontoon. Once it was in position above the rabbates, the valves could be opened and water would flow in until the deck rested on the rabbates. The valves could then be closed. The valves, operated from deck level, were under cast-iron covers in the footways.

Getting the water out again required rather more ingenuity: Mallet used the principle of the syphon. A pipe was fixed inside the hull of the pontoon; the inside floor of the pontoon sloped slightly so that water would flow towards the syphon.

A bell-ended pipe extended from the canal to the syphon device on the bank. Opening a valve started a flow of water from the canal; that flow in turn started the syphon effect, which extracted water from inside the pontoon. Once that happened, the flow from the canal could be cut off.

Mallet used the fact that the canal was 30 feet above the road to provide the difference in height required for the operation of a syphon. The only remaining problem, then, was that a flexible pipe was needed to make a temporary connection between the mechanism on the pontoon and that on the bank. Mallet used a hose: 'an intermediate flexible tube, formed of a spiral of hammer-hardened hoop iron, 6 inches in diameter'.

The hoop iron was covered by a sheet of gutta-percha, covered in turn by a leather coat to provide protection. Wikipedia says that 'Western inventors discovered the properties of gutta-percha latex in 1842'.[126] This lends credence to Mallet's claim that

the Author believes, that this was the first occasion upon which a continuous lining of gutta percha was thus applied, to any suction pipe, and he has found it to answer so perfectly that he has since applied it largely, and with success, to the suction-pipes of fire-engines.

Operation

MALLET said that the pontoon and syphon worked well. It cost £1,125, plus about £150 for masonry work, and was built between October 1846 and February 1847. It had been in continuous use up to December 1849 [when Mallet wrote his paper], 'giving perfect satisfaction'.

It needed only one man to operate it. Pumping out the water took only about three minutes; the whole operation of shifting it out of the way, to leave the canal open, took four minutes, and in three minutes the bridge could be back in position. As Mallet put it:

These operations may probably appear slow and troublesome, but the fact is, that the bridge in question, which is twice the width of roadway of any swivel bridge in Great Britain, is readily opened, leaving the space free for navigation in four minutes, and it can be closed again, and the roadway passage be made complete, in less than three minutes; being much less time than is usually required for moving common swivel bridges; and, if it was desirable, the time could be easily reduced.

Broadstone's later life

FILLING in the harbour meant that Broadstone itself was no longer involved with the canal after 1877. The Broadstone line gradually fell into disuse and, in 1927, the southern end was filled in; the northern end followed in 1956.[127]

In September 1933 the Lord Mayor of Dublin, Alderman Alfie Byrne TD, opened 'Dublin's new play centre', a 'boon for city children', a 'tasteful park that had now been laid out by the Corporation on what was some six years ago a canal waterway'. It included an enclosed area for children up to the age of fourteen, where they could play in safety. The Carnegie UK Trust had contributed £500 and the keys were presented to Mr Charles E. Jacob, Hon. Treasurer of the Civics Institute.[128] Making the park had provided work during a period of high unemployment – and the scheme preserved the line of the canal.

Between 1902 and 1911 the Dublin United Tramways Company and the MGWR discussed proposals for a tramway connecting the Broadstone station to the city centre, but no line was built and the station remained isolated. When the MGWR amalgamated with other lines in 1924/5 to form Great Southern Railways, maintenance of road vehicles was concentrated at Broadstone. All revenue-earning services at the station ended in 1937 but the site remained in use as a depot for steam engines until 1961. Broadstone is now used by the public service bus companies Dublin Bus and Bus Éireann.

The return of rail and the resurrection of the lye by

BUT rail is on its way back: the Luas light rail system's new Cross City line will run from Dublin city centre through Broadstone and then, on the old MGWR rail cutting, to Broombridge, which is on the Royal Canal and on the MGWR's line to the west.

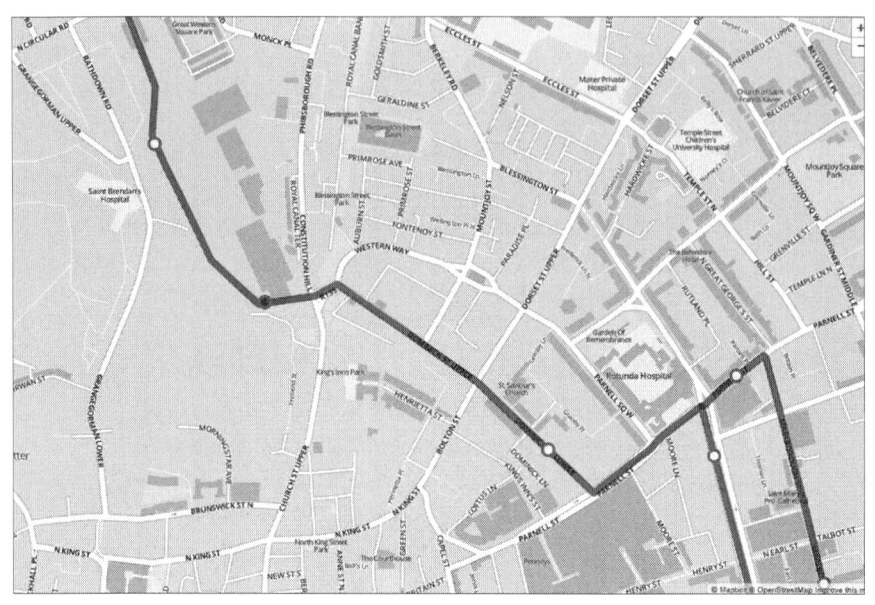

The Broadstone stop on the LUAS cross-city line
image courtesy of RPA/Luas Cross City

Excavating the lye by
image courtesy of RPA/Luas Cross City

The Railway Procurement Agency commissioned a series of archaeological investigations of surviving sub-surface remains at the Broadstone site. It is expected that field work will continue until 2015 but, during initial archaeological testing in 2010, three test trenches were excavated in the forecourt of the Broadstone building. Trench Two showed what was thought at first to be a slipway on the bank of the canal.[129] However, after additional testing and excavation in 2013 and 2014, the archaeologists now believe that this feature represents the remains of Mallet's 'lye by'.[130, 131]

SIX

Steam in the 1870s

Peter Clarke, Ruth Delany and Ernie Shepherd all describe the use of steamers on the canal in the 1870s. However, there may have been an earlier attempt at using steam. Lewis's *Topographical Dictionary* (1837) says this about the canal town of Mullingar:

The principal trade is in wool, for which this is the greatest mart in the county, its central situation and facility of communication with the Shannon and with Dublin having rendered it the commercial centre of a wide extent of country. The City of Dublin Steam Company commenced operations here in 1830: a steamer plies twice a week between this town and Shannon Harbour, where it meets the Limerick steamer and Grand Canal boat for Dublin.[132]

The City of Dublin Steam Packet Company ran paddle-steamers on the river Shannon, towing 'trade boats' (unpowered barges), mostly loaded with agricultural produce, to Shannon Harbour, where the Grand Canal meets the Shannon. From there, the trade boats were hauled by horse to the port in Dublin. The steamers were essentially tugs, but they also carried passengers, who used the Grand Canal Company's passage boats to get to Dublin. Some of the steamers were catamarans, with a single paddle wheel between two hulls, designed for use on canals.

The route that Lewis describes would have been a roundabout way of getting to Dublin. The steamer would have gone west on the canal and south on the Shannon, rather than directly eastward. The journey would have involved 37 miles and 21 locks on the canal to reach the Shannon, about 48 miles and three locks on the Shannon (including a crossing of Lough Ree) and then 82 miles and 43 locks on the Grand Canal – whereas the direct route would have involved only 52 miles and 25 locks. The route would have enabled the steamer to serve Longford, Tarmonbarry, Lanesborough and Athlone, but Lewis does not mention steamer services at any of those places other than Athlone. I have so far found no other mention of this service.

There is rather more information about the use of screw-steamers in the 1870s. Clarke, Delany and Shepherd give slightly different accounts; I have attempted here

The early 1870s MGWR steamers

SHEPHERD, in his *The Midland Great Western Railway of Ireland*, says that in 1870 the MGWR got an estimate from Grendons of Drogheda for a cargo steamer for use on the canal and then ordered two boats.[133] One of them was disabled by August 1871; the following March Courtney Stephens of Dublin were commissioned to fit new boilers by 1 May 1873. Steamer No.1 was out of action with a broken main shaft in March 1874; it is not clear whether this was the steamer with the new boilers or the other steamer.

Neither Clarke nor Delany mentions these early steamers, but the *Freeman's Journal* of 23 September 1870 provides supporting evidence from the Chairman's address at the previous day's half-yearly meeting of the MGWR:

As to the canal traffic, he begged to say that a very large class of goods could be carried by the canal at very great advantage to the company, if they had only the means of doing so. The first idea of having steamers on it arose from hearing that the Canadian weed which grew in the canal, and the removal of which cost a large sum in the year, could be cut by the action of steamers if placed in it. At present they paid 10d a ton for the carriage of coals. Now that could be done if they had their own steamers. The directors thought it desirable, therefore, to ask permission from the shareholders to purchase two of these, each of which would cost about £900.[134]

The *Irish Times* report of 22 September 1871 shows that the steamers had arrived. It reported the Chairman's address at the previous day's half-yearly meeting of the MGWR: 'He stated that the two steamers in operation on their canal were doing good work in ridding the canal of weeds'.[135]

I have found no MGWR advertisements offering to carry goods on these steamers, or to tow unpowered canal boats with them. It therefore seems likely that, if they were not just maintenance boats, they were used only for carrying the company's own supplies, especially coal from Dublin port.

The mid 1870s MGWR steamers

THERE is more agreement between the authors on the use of steamers from around 1875. Clarke and Delany agree that the MGWR began carrying in horse-drawn boats first. Clarke, citing the minutes of the evidence given to the Waterways Commission in 1923, says that in 1876 the company spent £5,000 buying four new screw steamers.[136] Delany says that the company bought five steamers in 1875: **Mermaid**, **Conqueror** and **Pioneer** were small tugs, towing three boats each; **Rambler** and **Rattler** could carry 30 tons each and had steam winches as well as steam engines.[137]

In her book *The Shannon Navigation* Delany says that the **Rambler** and **Rattler** were used on the river Shannon as well as on the Royal Canal.[138]

Former MGWR steamer Rambler
Author

Shepherd says that, in August 1876, Edward Hayes [of the Watling Works, Stony Stratford, Buckinghamshire] offered to provide a tug for £830; six months later he billed the company for the *Pioneer*. The *Mermaid* was ordered six months after that and was ready for inspection in May 1878. Hayes also supplied the *Rambler*.

The *Irish Times* of 8 September 1876 reported on the Chairman's address at the previous day's half-yearly meeting of the MGWR. Sir Ralph Cusack reported that the largest trader on the Royal Canal was about to retire from business because of ill health and that:

it might be very inconvenient to persons in the country, who carry on the canal materials that are not exactly suited for a railway, such as coals, timber, slates, bricks, etc ... it is therefore our intention to commence – perhaps in a small way at first – carrying with a couple of boats on the canal, so as to relieve the railway of this rough kind of traffic, and at the same time to benefit the country through which the canal runs.[139]

Sir Ralph said that the company had ordered a small steamer:

We don't propose that the steamer shall carry goods, but we propose to have a few small tugs similar to those used by Sir Arthur Guinness on the Liffey to draw laden boats ... we will begin in a small way and see what way the thing will do. We cannot lose very much by it. We are getting one small tug, and I suppose we will get another.[140]

The first steamer does not seem to have been suitable for the canal because, by March 1877, it was operating on the river Liffey instead. It may have been able to carry goods, not just to tow.

We expect to have delivered to-morrow a new steamer to run on the canal from this to Longford. The steamer we had before is engaged by agreement we made with the Messrs Guinness to carry their porter from the wharf opposite the Royal Barracks down to our docks such porter as is to be sent down by our rail. We are getting a new steamer more adapted to run on the canal with boats after them.[141]

The earliest advert I have found, offering the services of the canal steamers, was dated 11 October 1877.

The Company, having now placed on the Royal Canal several Barges drawn by Steamers, are prepared to enter into arrangements with Millers, Corn Factors, Timber and Potato merchants, &c, for the conveyance of grain, coal, timber, and other heavy consignments. All information as to rates can be obtained upon application to the Manager's Office, Broadstone.

J E Ward, Manager, Broadstone, 11th October, 1877.[142]

By March of the following year, the company had four steamers, with a fifth on order, as well as boats for carrying cattle and other goods. The company declined to compete with existing traders; provincial millers used the company's boats to carry their corn and the service was breaking even.[143] It seems that the company's steamer was no longer carrying Guinness on the river Liffey: porter was now carried by rail from Guinness's own yard to the Liffey Junction and distributed to the three railway companies, including the MGWR, that carried it from Dublin. That reduced congestion on the MGWR's quays.[144]

MGWR steamer operations

I have found no further information about the operation of the steamer fleet until 1884. By then at least one of the steamers had left the canal. On 26 July 1884 the *Irish Times* carried an article entitled 'The Western Coast and its Fisheries' in which the anonymous author reported that, at Westport on Ireland's Atlantic coast, an 'enterprising Englishman' had come over to instruct the natives in modern fishing techniques. However, Westport quay was six miles from the open sea, and the Englishman's steam trawler had to travel up there to discharge its cargo. The writer said:

In Clew Bay and Blacksod Bay the Midland Great Western Railway Company have placed one of their canal steam launches, which, although an old boat, is yet tolerably good for smooth water, but her steam power is too small and her pace too slow for the purposes for which she is intended – that of taking the fish from a regular steam trawler, and transmitting it to the railway terminus at Westport.[145]

I do not know which steam launch was sent to Co. Mayo or what happened to it afterwards.

In September and October 1884, MGWR adverts said:

Winter Service

From 1st October Next, and until further Notice, the Company's Trade Boats on the Royal Canal will only ply once each fortnight with Goods for Ballinacargy and Ballymahon, leaving the Spencer Dock every alternate Monday Morning, commencing the 6th October prox.

J E Ward, Manager
Broadstone Station, Dublin
8th September, 1884 [146]

There was no mention of any service to towns outside the eleven-mile stretch between Ballinacargy and Ballymahon: nothing to Mullingar (or anywhere eastward of it); nothing to Longford or to the river Shannon.

By 1886 the service was even more restricted: it no longer ran from Dublin. The steamer or steamers were based in Mullingar; goods were sent there by rail and then carried to Ballynacargy [the spelling had changed], Abbeyshrule and Ballymahon by boat. There were three sailings each way in a fortnight. The timetable showed sailings from Mullingar on 16, 20, 25 and 30 March; from Ballymahon on 18, 23 and 27 March.[147]

I found no announcement of an abandonment of the service but, in 1887, the Chairman of the rival Grand Canal Company implied that it had ended: 'Steam had also been tried on the Royal Canal, and also abandoned as unprofitable (hear, hear)'.[148]

Thereafter steam launches and steam dredgers are recorded as having used the canal but I know of no record of steam- or indeed of motor-powered carrying or haulage later in the nineteenth century.

Fishbourne clamant

THE MGWR were not the only operators of steamers on the Royal Canal in the 1870s. Fishbourne and Co were carriers, based in Dublin but with offices in Belfast, Cork and London and at the Curragh Camp, an army training establishment in County Kildare. In an 1875 advertisement, they offered to

receive and forward goods and parcels daily to all parts of the United Kingdom and Continents of Europe and America. Furniture removed by road or rail without packing. Goods called for on receiving notice, and stored on moderate terms.[149]

In a notice dated 11 November 1876 they complained that the Irish railway companies had imposed large increases in the rates charged for Fishbourne's furniture vans. They said that they were now sending their vans 'by road with horses where water was not practicable'. They added: 'Our arrangements for conveyance by water are not yet fully completed, but we trust soon will be'.[150]

Fishbournes had ordered traction engines and, in January 1877, they announced that the first of them had arrived, along with a wagon 'capable of carrying boilers and any such large consignment'. Furthermore, 'Our Express Steam Launches that we intend running to Athlone, Limerick, Mullingar, and Longford, are building, and we hope to have two ready against the 1st of March next'.[151]

Fishbournes intended to use the Royal Canal, which may explain why, in the same month, they were so strongly opposed to the MGWR's proposal to increase the canal tolls:

TO BOAT-OWNERS ON THE ROYAL CANAL

Get a copy of the Midland Railway Company's Bill that they are bringing into Parliament to enable them to double your tolls and charge you with dock dues.

COMBINE TOGETHER AND DEFEAT THEIR PROJECT.

As, if they are successful in passing it through Parliament, it will shut up the Canal, making it a Waterworks, and putting an end to Inland Navigation; and that, no doubt, is their intention.

The difference between Irish miles that they can only now charge, and English miles that they are going in for, together with an additional halfpenny, more than double the tolls on corn.

LAST DAY FOR LODGING PETITION, WEDNESDAY,
21st day of February.

For further particulars apply to Mr M'Combe, at Fishbourne's Office,
24 Bachelor's-walk, Dublin.[152]

Fishbournes worked with McCanns and other traders to oppose the MGWR bill.[153] In April they claimed a partial victory – while blaming the MGWR for the delayed start of the Fishbourne service:

Messrs Fishbourne and Co Have to apologise to the Gentry and Traders of the West of Ireland for not having their Steam Launches before this on the Royal Canal. But it was only last week the Railway Company abandoned that portion of their bill to increase the tolls on the Canal. The question of the depth of the water still remains undecided. We feel confident that the public will see no blame attaches to us, for until we can get a navigable depth of 4ft 6in for our launches it will be useless to think of putting them on. We have now brought the matter before the Board of Works, who have control over the Canal, and we feel confident that his Grace the Lord Lieutenant will see justice done.[154]

The MGWR, on the other hand, welcomed Fishbourne's advent: 'I understand Mr

Fishbourne is about running in opposition to us. We will be most happy when he does commence'.[155]

In June 1877 Fishbourne's advertised for an experienced traffic manager for their Royal Canal steam launches, offering a liberal salary 'partly on commission and partly permanent'.[156] However, it was not until August that operations began.

We beg to inform the public that we purpose running our Steam Launches from the Custom House quay, Dublin, commencing the 20th inst, and every Monday afternoon at 4 o'clock, with Cargo to Mullingar, Ballinacargy, Abbeyshrule, Ballymahon, Longford, Rooskey, Jamestown, and Carrick-on-Shannon, returning from Carrick-on-Shannon every Monday.[157]

The word 'launches' suggests that Fishbournes had acquired at least two vessels, and later adverts gave more details: one steamer was to leave Carrick-on-Shannon every Monday at noon and another would leave Custom House Quay, in Dublin, each Monday afternoon. The service extended beyond the Royal Canal to towns – Rooskey, Jamestown, Carrick-on-Shannon – on the northern (upstream) reaches of the river Shannon. Fishbournes had agents in Ballinacargy and Ballymahon towards the western end of the Royal Canal, Clondra at the junction with the Shannon and Carrick-on-Shannon on the north Shannon.[158]

Fishbournes maintained their aggressive attitude towards the MGWR. In September they placed placards complaining about the state of the canal; the MGWR Chairman responded at the company's half-yearly meeting, adding that Fishbournes had sent several letters of complaint:

a peculiarity of all of which was that the writer always travelled with his solicitor. 'I was travelling along the canal the other day with my solicitor;' 'I was delayed yesterday so long, but fortunately my solicitor was with me' (laughter), and so on.[159]

Fishbourne's service did not last long, as they announced in October 1877:

MESSRS FISHBOURNE & CO regret to inform the public that they are compelled to cease running their Steam Launches to Ballymahon, Carrick-on-Shannon, &c, in consequence of the state which the canal has been allowed to get into – choked with weeds and mud.

The propeller of their Launch, actually broken by railway sleepers lying in the mud, and all their efforts to hasten the action of the Irish Government who have a control over the Inland Navigation having proved unavailing, the matter must rest until the opening of Parliament.

As soon as the obstructions to the traffic on the canal are removed their Launches will commence running again.[160]

These notices appeared just as the MGWR announced its own steamer service on the canal.[161] Durkin and McCann, two of the largest traders on the canal, contradicted

Fishbourne's assertions about the state of the canal; an editorial in the *Freeman's Journal* was implicitly critical of Fishbourne.[162] The Fishbourne announcements were repeated throughout the winter but I have found no indication that the launches ever again ran on the Royal Canal.

The 1870s steamers: a combined list

SHEPHERD says that it is not clear how many vessels the MGWR owned and I have come to the same conclusion. The list of Royal Canal steamers might include:
— two steamers, names unknown, from Grendons of Drogheda, acquired in 1870 or 1871;
— the two tugs *Pioneer* and *Mermaid* supplied by Hayes of Stony Stratford in 1877 and 1878. *Pioneer* may have ended up in West Africa.[163] I have no information about *Mermaid;*
— the *Rambler*, built by Hayes in an unspecified year, which is still afloat in Ireland;
— the tug *Conqueror*, listed by both Delany and Shepherd, which was hired by a Mr Powderly in 1892. It may have been one of the two scrapped in 1916 or the one converted into an unpowered repair boat in 1920;
— the *Rattler*, listed by both Delany and Shepherd. I do not know who built it, where or when, or what happened to it. Shepherd found it listed in the traffic minutes; a Mr Lefroy wanted to hire it in 1890;
— the *Dauntless*, mentioned in 1908, again found by Shepherd in the traffic minutes. I have no more information about it;
— the two Fishbourne launches, about which I have no information.
There may be some overlap on that list; more research is needed.

There were trials of an experimental steamer on the Royal Canal in 1841: see Chapter 8.

SEVEN

Royal Canal bridges in Dublin

Ewan Duffy

CONVENTION holds that the Royal Canal opened in 1796 from the harbour at Broadstone to Kilcock with subsequent westward extensions to bring it to the river Shannon and eastward from Phibsboro to the North Wall in Dublin, where the canal locked down into the river Liffey.[164] Nothing further of interest from a construction or archaeological viewpoint applies. Except that this is not the case.

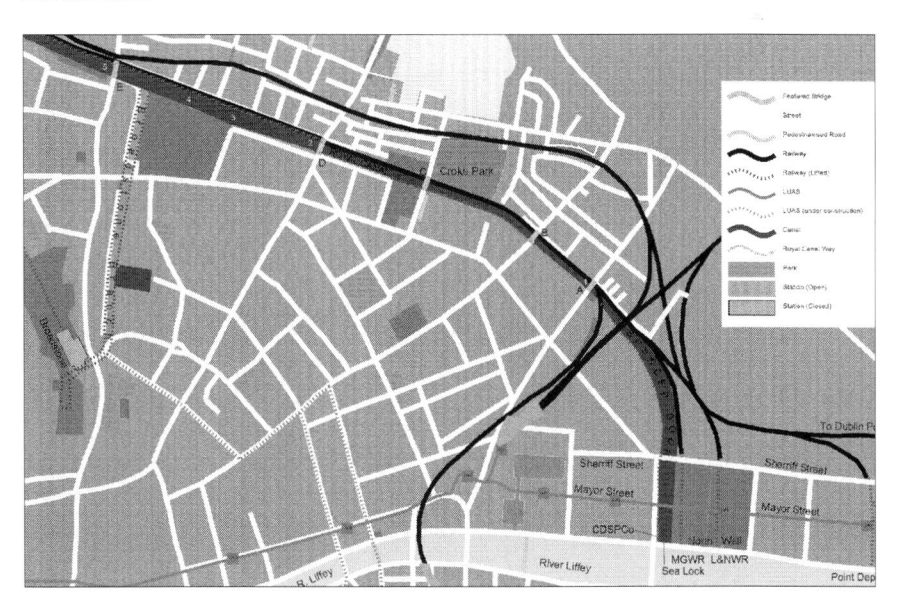

The Royal Canal in Dublin
© *www.industrialheritageireland.info*

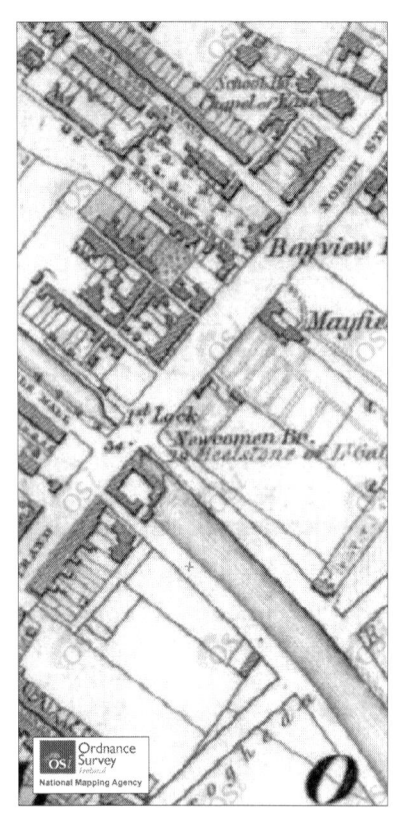

Newcomen Bridge

A look at the first edition Ordnance Survey map for the area inland from the sea lock at the river Liffey shows that the 1st Lock was located to the east of Newcomen Bridge. A visit to the area today will show the 1st Lock on the west side of Newcomen Bridge. What happened?

In the 1870s, the Midland Great Western Railway [MGWR] carried out a major redevelopment of the area between the Sea Lock and Newcomen Bridge, creating Spencer Dock in the process. This allowed for effective transhipment of goods from sea to rail or canal and vice versa. As part of this process, a siding was installed on the west side of the new dock, which also served the premises of the City of Dublin Steam Packet

left: 1st Lock below Newcomen Bridge
below: 1st Lock above Newcomen Bridge
Ordnance Survey Ireland

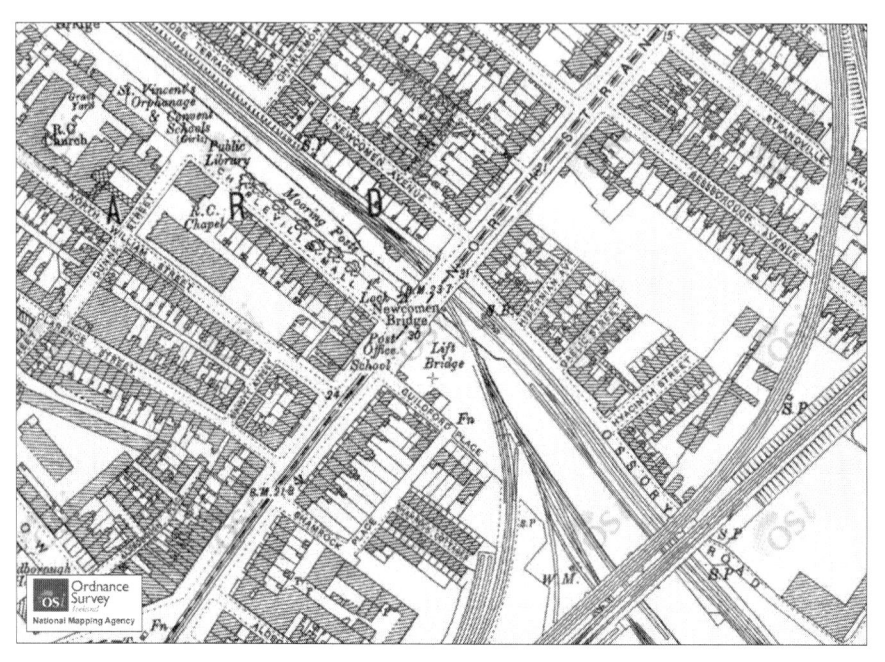

Newcomen Bridge
© www.industrialheritageireland.info

Company. This opened for service in 1872. As the siding was on the opposite side of the dock to the MGWR's Liffey Line (opened in March 1864), a lifting bridge over the canal was required to allow for connection of the new siding to the Liffey Line. As the 1st Lock was in the way, it was removed and a new 1st Lock was built on the western side of Newcomen Bridge.

All well and good: problem solved, except that this throws up a conundrum. When the 1st Lock was east of Newcomen Bridge, the canal level above the lock would be too high to allow boats to pass under Newcomen Bridge.

Checking the historic Ordnance Survey maps online, the first edition map [Historic 6"] shows a spot height of 34 feet.[165] The later edition [Historic 25"] shows a spot height at 30 feet south of the bridge and 31 feet north of the bridge – but no height on the bridge itself. This suggests that the bridge was rebuilt or lowered by 3–4 feet between the first edition 6" and the later 25" map. That would explain why the lock had to be moved to the west side of the bridge, where it now resides. So why was the bridge rebuilt? The answer to the bridge spot height difference lies in Dublin's tramway history.

The Dublin Tramways Company obtained its first Act of Parliament in 1871; it authorised – among other things – a line from the city to Dollymount. This line crossed Newcomen Bridge, which was lowered to ease the gradient for tramway traffic.[166] The *Irish Times* of 14 March 1873 recorded the opening of the tram line to Dollymount (via Clontarf).[167] Notwithstanding this easing of the gradient on the approaches to the bridge, trace horses were still required here to assist in the passage of trams. The Police Regulations under the Dublin Traffic Act 1875 specified a number of locations where horses were required to be up to the job of hauling their laden vehicles without the risk of injury to the animals concerned. Newcomen Bridge was one of only two tramway locations so cited.[168]

There was another interesting aspect to the rebuilding of Newcomen Bridge. At the time that these developments were taking place, Dublin Corporation were in the process of establishing a main drainage scheme for the city (the Main Drainage Company). The rebuilding at a lower height of Newcomen Bridge over the Royal Canal and the adjacent railway bridge on the Liffey Line was coordinated with the laying of the Main Drainage sewer/siphon, which passes underneath.

Finally, there is one other factor which would have made the canal unable to fit under the present Newcomen Bridge: the level of the canal. Above the 1st Lock, this was raised from its original height. The *Irish Times* of 12 October 1875 reports on a meeting of Dublin Corporation where it was advised that it was necessary for the purposes of the railway company (MGWR) that the level of the canal at this point should become higher.[169]

Remains of original 1st Lock
© *www.industrialheritageireland.info*

Clarke Bridge
© www.industrialheritageireland.info

Other bridges

HAVING found such strong evidence that Newcomen Bridge had been altered, and having identified the reason for that, the next step was to look at the other bridges over the canal which had tramways on them. However, something else was at play here. Above Newcomen Bridge as far as Westmoreland Bridge at Crossguns, most of the bridges were raised, not lowered.

The primary source for the determination of this fact was again the differences in spot heights between the 6" and later 25" Ordnance Survey maps. I initially considered this to show a reworking of the mean sea level; however, the benchmark heights of the canal locks above Binns Bridge remained the same between the two editions.

Clarke Bridge (Summerhill)

THE next bridge above Newcomen is Clarke Bridge at Summerhill. There is no evidence of the bridge or road having been raised or altered and in fact there is a clear delineation between the railway bridge and the canal bridge which suggests completely different periods of construction. In addition, the railway is at a lower level than the canal at this point (about 7.5m from the railway bridge parapet to the track compared with about 5m from the canal bridge parapet to the towpath).

A point of interest to note is the low level of the springing of the bridge arch. This is due to the raising of the canal level as noted previously.

Russell Street Bridge

THE next bridge over the canal is Russell Bridge, which was not present when the canal opened.[170] Frederick 'Buck' Jones, owner of the nearby Clonliffe House, arranged to have the bridge built after a friend drowned in the canal whilst heading across country from Clonliffe House to get back to the city, the nearest bridges at the time being Binns Bridge to the west and Clarke Bridge to the east. The road from Clonliffe Road to the bridge was called Buck Jones's Road, later becoming Jones's Road.[171] A map of Dublin City in 1818 shows the bridges on the Royal Canal as Newcomen Bridge and Clarke Bridge. What is now Russell Street is marked on the map but without a bridge nor Jones's Road to the north.[172] A map of the city in 1836 shows Jones's Road and Russell Bridge.[173] This narrows down the date of building of the bridge to some extent.

The first edition Ordnance Survey 6" map reports a bridge height of 37 feet. There is also a spot height of 42 feet at the junction between Russell Street and the North Circular Road. There are no spot heights or benchmarks for this location on the Ordnance Survey 25" map. With a drop of 5 feet shown between the Russell Street/North Circular Road junction and the bridge, you would expect to see evidence on the ground but there is no noticeable drop. However, there is quite a noticeable drop between the bridge and the Jones Road/Clonliffe Road junction to the north.

There is one other point to be observed here. To the east of Russell Street, there is a parallel street at a lower level called Saint Patrick's Terrace. The difference in height between its level and that of Russell Street is about 7 feet. It is my opinion that this is at the level of the original Russell Street. This would allow for the road to have

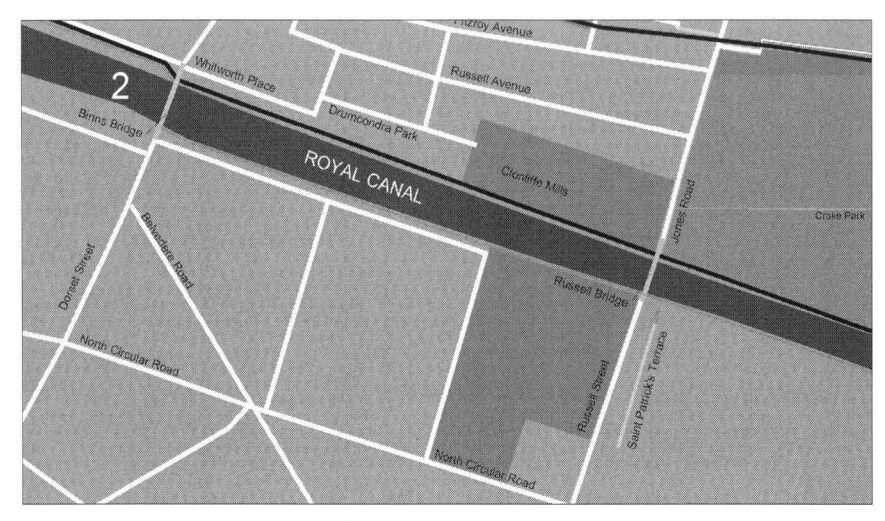

Saint Patrick's Terrace and Russell Street Bridge
© *www.industrialheritageireland.info*

Russell Street Bridge
© www.industrialheritageireland.info

fallen to 35 feet south of the bridge followed by a rise of about two feet for the arch of the original bridge. I believe that the bridge was rebuilt in the early 1860s as the railway and canal are at the same level at this point. However, the canal bridge was altered at a later date, perhaps in connection with a change in gradient of the road.

The one other observation I have is that the height of the springing is very low and there are minimal ropemarks on the bridge. As with Clarke Bridge, this is due to the raising of the level of the canal in the 1870s.

Binns Bridge and 2nd Lock

THE next bridge is Binns Bridge. The plaque on the bridge, stating 'Binns Bridge 1793', appears to be original. However, the Ordnance Survey 6" map gives a benchmark height for the keystone of 44 feet, the 25" map a benchmark for the road of 50.3 feet. At Crossguns Bridge, the map shows a two foot difference between keystone and road height; I would allow the same for Binns Bridge. This suggests a raising of the bridge by about four feet.

There is another piece of evidence that the bridge was raised. On the adjacent Whitworth Place (on the north east side of Binns Bridge), houses have a basement below the level of the road. If we consider that Binns Bridge was lower than today, Whitworth Place would also have been lower. The first part of Whitworth Place is shown on the first edition (6") Ordnance Survey map. When Binns Bridge was raised, Whitworth Place had to be similarly raised in order to maintain connection to the Drumcondra Road at its new higher level. The houses in Whitworth Place were present before the road was raised. It is likely that they were accessed at first-floor level, as today, but by means of steps from the lower road level. At its present (raised) level, the first floor of these houses is at the same height as the road.[174] The houses in Drumcondra Park were built at a later date and the ground has been raised in line with the new level of Whitworth Place. This can be seen by looking into the site of the former Clonliffe Mills, which is at a lower level than the adjacent houses.

The 2nd Lock of the canal (a double lock/staircase pair) is partially under Binns Bridge and here the interesting bit starts. The lower lock chamber appears to have been extended as there are recesses for the lock gates under the bridge.

At road level, the bridge is quite wide, which suggests that it has been widened. I was not able to find a join as the underside of the canal bridge has been gunnited.[175] However, the railway bridge provides clear evidence of a join in the two parts of the bridge arch on the Up line. This is slightly less than half way in (about 45%) from the west face to the east face of the bridge. As such, it would appear that the bridge was widened on the east side and in fact more than doubled in width. The railway line opened in 1864, which would suggest that the bridge was widened after 1864.

This would also explain the lock gate recesses under the bridge: they would not have been under the original bridge but when it was widened on the downstream side, it was necessary to extend the lock to leave the lower gates beyond the bridge. The original recesses would fit in with the canal bridge having been widened from about 45% of its present width (starting from the west face) to its present width.

When did this occur? As with Newcomen Bridge being altered for tramway development, the approaches to Binns Bridge were altered in the 1870s for the tramline to Drumcondra.[176] However, that would not have required a widening of the bridge. The Drumcondra Road was widened around 1930; I would suggest that this is the period when Binns Bridge was widened.[177] This gives Binns Bridge three phases of development: initial bridge, raised bridge and widened bridge.

Above Binns Bridge

ABOVE Binns Bridge, the canal passes through two further locks (3rd and 4th). The benchmarks on these are the same between the two maps, which assisted greatly in ruling out a recalibration of the Ordnance Survey base level. The MGWR Liffey line is in a cutting to the north of the canal and to the north of this is Whitworth Road. The road was built as a means of avoiding the toll on the Drumcondra Turnpike, which was located about a quarter of a mile north of Binns Bridge. Traffic would cross the bridge and turn left to get to Crossguns before continuing north on the Ashbourne Road.[178] All turnpikes still in operation in Ireland were abolished under the Dublin and Other Roads Turnpike Abolition Act 1855. The first day of toll-free operation under the Act was 5 January 1856.[179]

Both the canal and the railway bridge at Crossguns and 5th Lock have been widened by means of non-masonry extensions on the downstream side (the railway section was renewed again in 2012). On the os 6" map, the road level is given as 94 feet (keystone 92 feet). On the os 25" map, the west face has a benchmark of 99.1 and the east face 97.7! As at the 2nd lock, the presence of recesses for the former gate location provides evidence of the lock having been lengthened.

Why?

WHY were the bridges rebuilt, but not the intermediate (3rd and 4th) locks? Railway history appears to have the answer. In 1859 the MGWR obtained Parliamentary sanction to build a railway line from Liffey Junction to the Liffey Quays at the North Wall. Colloquially known as the Liffey Line, this line curved away from the MGWR mainline at Liffey Junction in Cabra before curving back in to parallel the Royal Canal, which was owned by the MGWR.

In the days before the super cruiser, the clearance required under a canal bridge was lower than that required by a railway line. As the railway parallels the canal between the 1st and 5th locks, road bridges over the railway would need to be at a height sufficient to allow trains to pass underneath. By 1859, when the MGWR obtained their Act of Parliament, the Board of Trade – as the civil service department responsible for regulating railways – had had time to develop its pathological hatred of level crossings. It would not have permitted the option of raising the bed of the railway and having level crossings at Phibsboro, Drumcondra Road, Russell Street, Summerhill and North Strand Road.[180]

Looking back at my analysis of the bridges above, I mentioned the relative height of the railway at each location. It is my belief that the construction of the Liffey Line required the adjacent canal bridges to be raised or rebuilt to allow for a smooth road passage across the railway and canal at each location, whilst maintaining sufficient clearance under the railway bridges and minimising the gradient for the railway. The Liffey Line is on a continuous decline for its length. At Liffey Junction (7th Lock), it is above the level of the canal. However, east of Newcomen Junction, the railway and canal are separated by only a few feet in height, despite the canal having fallen through six locks.

The one corroborating piece of evidence in favour of this conclusion is a Letter to the Editor of the *Irish Times* in October 1863, complaining about the state in which the MGWR's contractor had left the road and footpath at Binns Bridge The writer said: 'it was necessary to form an arch in connexion with the Canal Bridge, since which, although several months have elapsed, there appears to be no notion on the part of the contractor to put it in that state of repair in which it was previously'.[181]

To summarise, the MGWR had to choose whether to raise three canal bridges or to lower the trackbed of their railway even further, with the negative consequences of steeper gradients and the greater cost of extracting more material.

EIGHT

Watson's Double Canal Boat

THERE is no record (that I know of) of the reaction of canal boatmen to the approach of a 120-foot long, very narrow, steam-powered boat on the Royal Canal in 1841. I suspect, though, that its manoeuvres caused no little surprise.

The City of Dublin Steam Packet Company

THIS steamer was an experimental passenger-carrying boat designed by William Watson, manager of the inland department of the City of Dublin Steam Packet Company [CODSPCO]. The company operated on the Irish Sea, on the Shannon Estuary and on the non-tidal part of the river Shannon, upstream of the town of Killaloe.

The estuary steamers carried passengers and cargo whereas the river steamers were tugs, which towed 'trade boats' (barges) carrying cargoes; passengers travelled on board the tugs. However, the steamers did not travel on the 15-mile Limerick Navigation that linked the city of Limerick, at the head of the Shannon Estuary, to the steamer route upstream of Killaloe. On that navigation, the trade boats were towed by horses; passengers travelled in a separate horse-drawn boat.

By 1840, the company had three years' experience of operating an innovative vessel, the *Nonsuch* horse-drawn iron passage boat, on that navigation:[182]

a sheet-iron boat, 80 feet long and 6 feet 6 inches wide at midships, having the stem and stern ends (each 10 feet long) attached by strong hinges to the body, and susceptible of being rapidly raised to a vertical position by means of winches; thus reducing the length to 60 feet when required to pass through a lock ... The weight of one man at each end is amply sufficient to keep down the ends when the boat is in motion.[183]

The whole of that 60 feet was available for carrying passengers:

it is capable of carrying 60 passengers, travelling at a speed of 9 miles per hour, with the same power that was required to draw a 60 feet boat with a less load, and there is a much less action on the canal bank in consequence of the increased length, which at the same time imparts stiffness, and enables passengers to enter and leave the boat with safety.

Considerable time is saved in passing the locks, by the opposition of the square end when the bow is raised; the boat may thus be run almost at full speed into the lock, and both ends being raised simultaneously, it is stopped much more easily than if the tapered ends were down.[184]

Saunders's News Letter said that the company wanted to introduce

a steam-boat of larger dimensions, giving greater comfort and accommodation to passengers, with greater safety, and capable of being wrought at less cost than the fly-boat. Until, however, a recent period, the many obstacles that beset the difficult problem of steam navigation on narrow canals had precluded the possibility of this.[185]

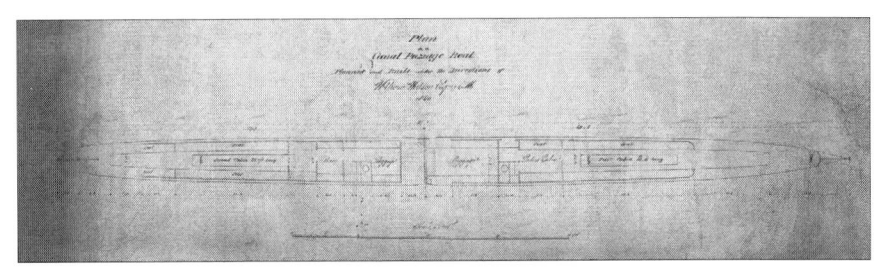

Watson's Canal Passage Boat
courtesy The Waterways Archive/Canal and River Trust

The inventive Mr Watson

In March 1838 William Watson patented 'an improved boat or vessel to be used on canal and other inland navigations'.[186]

The design reflected the idea that a light, long, narrow boat could travel faster, or with less horsepower, than a wider boat. However, the length was restricted by the size of the locks that the boat had to pass through.

The *Nonsuch*, with its bow and stern that could be raised, was designed to overcome that restriction; Watson proposed to go much further, with a boat very much longer than the *Nonsuch*. The shortest lock on the Limerick Navigation was only 79 feet long, but Watson's boat was almost 120 feet. As *The Mechanics' Magazine* put it:

Mr Watson's principal improvement in boats for inland navigation consists in constructing them in such manner, as that they may be temporarily shortened whenever occasion requires, and be thus enabled to pass through lock-chambers of less length than the boats themselves are when fully extended.[187]

There were two variants of the design. With the first, the boat would have been built in three watertight sections, hinged vertically. At a lock, the two ends of the boat would have been folded back alongside the main part of the hull but would not have been detached. The folding would have required a very wide stretch of canal outside each end of the lock. I have found no evidence that this variant was ever built.

The second variant was more straightforward, consisting of just two sections, connected by coupling links and bolts and then separated for passing through locks. There is a drawing of just such a boat in the Waterways Archive at the Canal & River Trust's National Waterways Museum at Ellesmere Port in Cheshire.[188] It is headed 'Plan of a Canal Passage Boat planned and built under the directions of William Watson Esqre AM 1840'.

It seems unlikely that two William Watsons designed 120-foot canal passenger boats at around the same time, so I think that this is the boat designed by Watson of the CODSPCO. This variant was built (although I do not know who built it) and tested on the Royal Canal.

Sources of information

I have found two accounts of the boat and its trials. *The Mechanics' Magazine* carried a brief notice in November 1841 and an article, reproduced from *Saunders's News Letter*, in December 1841.[189] Further information was provided in 1866 by Robert Mallet, in a contribution to a discussion at the Institution of Civil Engineers.[190]

The original account in *The Mechanics' Magazine* of 1839 said nothing about the propulsion of the canal boat, but *Saunders's News Letter* said that it was to be a steam boat. Mallet, who had helped to introduce Scottish-style horse-drawn fast passenger boats on both the Royal and the Grand Canal, said that he was asked 'to adapt steam power and paddle wheels to this boat, in place of horse power', which suggests that it was originally designed as a horse-drawn boat. The drawing in the Waterways Archive, dated 1840, supports that interpretation: it does not show any provision for engines, boiler or paddle wheels.

Saunders's News Letter said that the boat was intended for use on the Limerick Navigation, between Limerick and Killaloe, 'the only point [on the Shannon] where the circumstances of the navigation have hitherto prevented the use of steam vessels'. Mallet, however, said that it was for use on the Grand and Royal Canals:

[Watson was] thus interested in improving the passenger boats on the canals in the hands of the Canal Companies, and of ascertaining how far this could be effected by the substitution of steam power for that of horses ... The conditions of the problem were, that if a speed of about 8 miles an hour could be obtained, with a cargo of sixty passengers and their luggage, so that the journey from Dublin to Shannon Harbour could be made in one day, it would be a success; and it was believed it would then answer commercially.[191]

Shannon Harbour is the point at which the Grand Canal meets the river Shannon. The Grand and Royal canal companies carried passengers on their own canals; the CODSPCO did not carry passengers on those canals (though it carried cargoes on them).

The boat

Saunders's said that the boat was 120 feet long and that, when divided, the two sections could pass side by side through a lock 70 feet long. Mallet said that the boat's beam was 5ft 9in. Separating and rejoining the sections took two men only 40 seconds, using

a peculiar construction and mechanism of great simplicity, which is such that whatever be the difference of draught in each when separate, they are brought to an equal immersion when rejoined, and in fact become one rigid and firm boat.[192]

The forward section accommodated 60 passengers and up to one cwt of luggage each. At the time the *Saunders's* article was written, the boat was 'receiving her cabin furniture and fittings'; the trials were made using ballast to match the expected weight of the passengers.

The rear section carried two 30hp non-condensing steam engines, with a tubular (locomotive) boiler, the whole weighing less than five tons. Mallet said that they were high-pressure engines, capable of being wrought up to 40hp.

The boat had two paddle wheels, using modified versions of the oval floatboards patented by George Rennie, which dipped point first into the water; Mallet said that they 'were then believed to possess some peculiar properties in going easily into the water and lifting very little of it.' The helmsman steered using a wheel on deck between the paddle wheels and over the engine room, which gave him a good view, and there was a rudder 'of a peculiar construction, placed beneath the keel of the boat, to prevent injury by grounding on the sloping banks of the canal'.[193]

Mallet disliked the design:

The boat was of such extremely small beam ... so crank and so flimsy in build, that there was great difficulty in putting adequate power into her, or in obtaining sufficient foothold for machinery in a boat of such length, built of half-inch oak planking ... The weights were distributed, by the aid of longitudinal trussed keelsons, over as large a floor as possible, to enable the boat to sustain them.[194]

The heights of the bridges restricted the diameter of the paddle wheels; the widths of the locks restricted the size of the paddle floats. It is not clear where the wheels were fitted and how they affected the combined width when the two parts of the boat were alongside one another in a lock; perhaps the wheels were at the forward end of the rear section.

The trials

THE *Saunders's* report said: 'Lengthened and careful experiments have been made with this steam boat, as to speed and management, &c, on the six mile level of the Royal Canal – running measured distances'.[195]

This might refer to the 7.5 mile level [pound] from the 12th Lock at Blanchardstown to the 13th at Deey Bridge: it is close to Dublin and to Mallet's Victoria Foundry.[196] However, it is not clear where the boat sections could be turned at the Deey end.

Saunders's said that the boat was easy to manage, especially in locks: reversing the engines could stop the boat in its own length so check-ropes were not needed. The engines used 114lb of coke per hour, including that used in getting up steam.

Mallet said that the boat was tried upon both canals, the Grand as well as the Royal, and on 'the comparatively open waters of the [river] Liffey, at the port of Dublin, where she attained an estimated speed of about 10 miles an hour'; *Saunders's* said that in open water 'her speed has been found to reach as high as nine-and-a-half to ten miles per hour'.

On the canals, *Saunders's* said that, with crew, ballast and enough coke for the journey, the boat's speed was 'between six and seven British miles per hour'; it said that, on the Limerick Navigation, partially river and partially canal, the boat's average speed would be at least 7mph. Mallet, rather more precise, said:

With a load equivalent to sixty passengers and their baggage, a maximum speed of 7.08 miles an hour was attained, with the original oval float boards, 24 inches deep and 17 inches wide, and with the engines working considerably below their full speed.[197]

According to Mallet, the trials were quite extensive, including different types, sizes and shapes of paddle floats, different radii of paddle arms and different dips. The floats included the feathering oar-shaped floats invented by John Oldham and patented with the assistance of Charles Wye Williams, founder of the CODSPCO. With conventional floats, a wave went at an angle of 30° 'from the tail of each paddle wheel towards the bank' and was reflected several times, 'producing a set of waves crossing in a lattice form'. However, the feathering floats produced a surge across the canal, with a continuously breaking wave not far from the stern.

Mallet even tried providing equine assistance:

One curious experiment was made by attaching three picked and powerful fast post horses to the steam-boat, capable of keeping a strong strain upon the tow line while the engines were at work. On one occasion he started the engines and four horses at the same time, when the speed of the boat was rapidly brought up to 10 miles an hour, and that rate was maintained for perhaps 300 yards or 400 yards, the engines flying away and the horses being scarcely able to make speed enough to keep the tow lines taut. The true wave of translation was now soon produced, upon which the boat for a short time rode. This increased in magnitude, and very soon brought down the speed of the boat to its own rate, or to 8 miles an hour. Throwing off the horses when the speed was highest, it was almost immediately reduced to about 5 miles an hour, and until the water got tranquil could not be restored.[198]

Saunders's and Mallet agreed that the boat could reach 6mph on either canal, 'without notable disturbance'. The boat reached 7mph with the engines at half power; working up to full power produced more surge along the sides and at the rear but did not cause the boat to move faster.

Saunders's said that, if the boat could travel 24 miles in one day …

and allowing 10 per cent, for interest of capital in boat, complete wear and tear, repairs, wages of crew, &c, the total cost of transit of 60 passengers and luggage, per mile, is ten pence and a fraction, without any injury to the banks, or wear and tear upon the towing paths.[199]

Saunders's clearly thought the experiments a success and said that, after being fitted out, the boat would shortly proceed to her station on the Shannon by way of the Grand Canal. However if, as Mallet said, the intention was to achieve a speed of 8mph, then the experiments failed. Except on the open water of the Liffey, the boat never achieved more than 7.08 miles an hour under its own steam.

What became of the boat?

I have not yet found any record of the boat entering service on the Limerick Navigation. That is probably just as well, because it would have been a very dangerous vessel. For the first two [Irish] miles [2½ statute miles] above Limerick, the towing-path and the boatstream of the Limerick Navigation are on the south bank of a canal and then of the river Shannon. Then the navigation is continued in a stillwater canal whose entrance is on the north bank of the river. Watson's very long, very narrow boat would have had to cross the river, beam-on to the full force of the Shannon, at the foot of the Falls of Doonass.

But there is another intriguing possibility. In an article in the *Dublin Historical Record* in 1996, about No.25 Fitzwilliam Place in Dublin, Ireland, Roseanne Dunne said that the house first appeared in directories in 1843, when it was occupied by one William Watson, of whom she wrote:

In 1843 he became a director of the City of Dublin Steam Packet Co. Before this he had devised a canal passenger barge which was subsequently bought by the Egyptian Government.[200]

She provided no more information and I have not been able to find the sources she used. But it is not impossible, nor even implausible, that Watson's boat might have ended up in Egypt.[201]

In 1840 a new company, the Peninsular and Oriental Steam Navigation Company [P&O], had just been awarded a contract to carry the mails from the United Kingdom to the port of Alexandria, in Egypt. From there the mails were carried overland to Suez on the Red Sea, where they were picked up by a steamer and carried to India. Passengers travelled more slowly on the Overland Route: first on the Mahmoudié Canal from Alexandria to the Nile, then on the Nile itself to Cairo, then across the desert to Suez. The Suez Canal was not opened until 1869.

The P&O did not itself operate the Overland Route but it had a keen interest in its success – as did the Egyptian government, which took over the operation of the route in 1846. According to Freda Harcourt, in early 1841 James Hartley, who was (amongst many other things) a founder-director of the P&O, 'set up a small company to provide horse-drawn trackboats on the [Mahmoudié] canal.' It was an independent concern, 'probably to stand in on the transit' until the P&O could make more permanent arrangements, and he sold the boats to P&O in 1842.[202] Halford Lancaster Hoskins says that a small independent company had been operating horse-drawn track-boats on the canal 'for some time' and that J.R. Hill & Co. bought it in 1842, thus gaining complete control of the route from Alexandria to Suez.[203] Although Harcourt says that the boats were bought by the P&O and Hoskins that they were bought by J.R. Hill & Co., it is possible that they are talking about the same transaction.

The first horse-drawn track-boat was on the canal before November 1839.[204] A second track-boat arrived in June 1841:

The [P&O steamer] **Oriental** *had brought out from England a floating omnibus 105 feet long, for the purpose of conveying the mails and passengers on the Mahmoudieh Canal between Alexandria and the Nile, where they will be transferred to the* **Lotus** *iron steamer.*[205]

In November 1841, **PS Oriental** delivered at Alexandria 'a better adapted track boat than the previous ones sent out by Peninsular and Oriental Company for Hill & Co.', which suggests, first, that there were now at least three track-boats on the canal and, second, that P&O had been supplying Hill.[206]

Without its engines, Watson's boat would have been a horse-drawn passenger-carrying track-boat; separating it into two sections would have made it easier to transport on the deck of a steamer. And it is not impossible that Watson's boat would have come to the attention of the P&O line's directors.

James Hartley was one of them: he was a Dublin man, and a partner with the Bourne family in a Dublin coach-building business; Richard Bourne, of that family, was probably the most important of the P&O line's founder directors. But the directors also included Charles Wye Williams, Francis Carleton and Joseph Christopher Ewart, all of the City of Dublin Steam Packet Company.

I have not been able to prove that Watson's boat did or did not end up in Egypt but it is not impossible that a boat tested at Blanchardstown, on the Royal Canal, entered service on the Mahmoudié Canal in Alexandria.

Notes and references

Chapter 1: The Royal and Grand Canals

1. Waterways Ireland website checked June 2014, www.waterwaysireland.org

2. Railway Commissioners, *Second report of the Commissioners appointed to consider and recommend a general system of Railways for Ireland* HMSO 1838. Session 1837–8, Cmd 145, Vol.35, p.449

3. I have rounded the mileage and tonnage figures

4. Rounded

5. Year not stated; probably 1835

6. I have used the sterling pound £ symbol, rather than the italic *l*, and standardised the representation of shillings and pence throughout. There were 20 shillings in £1, 12 pennies in a shilling, so 240 pennies in a pound.

7. Railway Commissioners, op.cit

8. *The Freeman's Journal*, 10 September 1833

9. Ruth Delany and Ian Bath, *Ireland's Royal Canal 1789–2009*, The Lilliput Press, Dublin 2010

10. *The Freeman's Journal*, 5 December 1833

11. *The Freeman's Journal*, 6 September 1837

12. W.E. (Ernie) Shepherd, *The Midland Great Western Railway of Ireland: an illustrated history*, Midland Publishing Ltd, Leicester 1994

13. *The Freeman's Journal*, 2 December 1848

14. Ruth Delany, *The Grand Canal of Ireland*, David & Charles, Newton Abbot, 1973

15. Delany, op.cit

16. Railway Commissioners, op.cit, Appendix B, Nos 6 and 7

17. The Railway Commissioners used the term 'Lower Shannon' to mean the estuary, 60 miles long, with Limerick at its head. The 'Limerick Navigation', 15 miles of river and canal, linked Limerick to Killaloe, at the foot of Lough Derg. That lake was ignored in the Commissioners' categorisation. The 'Middle Shannon' was from Portumna to Athlone; Lough Ree, like Lough Derg, was ignored. Finally, the 'Upper Shannon' was from Lanesborough, at the head of Lough Ree, to Lough Allen

18. Thomas Rhodes CE, 'Third Report upon the present state of the River Shannon, and its Navigation, showing the Means of Improvement; also of reducing the Flood Waters near to the ordinary Summer Level, to facilitate the Drainage of the Lands and Bogs in its vicinity' in *Letter from Colonel John F. Burgoyne to the Right Hon Sir John Cam Hobhouse, Bart; and further Reports of Mr Rhodes, on the Improvement of the Navigation of the River Shannon*, Ordered, by the House of Commons to be printed, 10 June 1833

19. *Sailing Directions for the Lower Shannon, and for Lough Derg; with some Hydrographic Notices of Lough Ree and Lough Erne. By Commander James Wolfe RN; being the result of Surveys made by Order of the Lords Commissioners of the Admiralty*

20. ADM 344/345, 344/346 and 344/347 in *Records of the Admiralty, Naval Forces, Royal Marines, Coastguard, and related bodies* at The National Archives, Kew www.nationalarchives.gov.uk checked June 2014

21. Henry Boylan (ed), *A Dictionary of Irish Biography*, 3rd ed, Gill & Macmillan, Dublin, 1999 and 'Weld, Isaac' at *Dictionary of National Biography, 1885–1900, Vol.60* online at https://en.wikisource.org/wiki/Weld,_Isaac_(DNB00), checked June 2014

22. 'An Account of the First Steam Voyage on the British Seas, performed by the *Thames* steam-packet, from Glasgow to London, in the year 1815', in *Fraser's Magazine for Town and Country* September 1848 in Vol.XXXVIII, July to December 1848, John W. Parker, London

23. Isaac Weld, *Statistical Survey of the County of Roscommon, drawn up under the directions of the Royal Dublin Society*, Dublin 1832

24. Charles Wye Williams, *Observations on an important feature in the state of Ireland, and the want of employment of its population: with a description of the navigation of the river Shannon; suggested by the report of the select committee of the House of Commons on the state of the poor in Ireland, and the remedial measures proposed by them*, T. Vacher, Westminster 1831

Chapter 2: Sea ports, roads and markets

25. The modern equivalents of these roads are the M4/N4 from Dublin to Sligo, the M4/M6/N6 from Dublin to Galway and the M4/N4/N5 to Westport.

26. Weld mixed Irish and 'English' miles, sometimes saying which unit he was using and sometimes not doing so. Elsewhere, he gives the distance from Strokestown to Sligo as 34 miles Irish, a little over 43 miles English

27. Rhodes, op.cit

28. *Thom's Irish Almanac and Official Directory, with the Post Office Dublin City and County Directory, for the year 1850…*, Alexander Thom, Dublin; Longman, Brown, Green, and Longmans, London; Adam and Charles Black, Edinburgh 1850

29. Weld citing Charles Wye Williams op.cit. By 1850 Liverpool was importing 90 million eggs a year from Ireland; in total Ireland contributed 500 million eggs of the total British annual consumption of about 1.5 billion eggs. Source: Braithwaite Poole, *Statistics of British Commerce, being a Compendium of the Productions, Manufactures, Imports, and Exports, of the United Kingdom, in Agriculture, Minerals, Merchandise, &c, &c, &c,* W.H. Smith & Son and Simpkin, Marshall & Co, London; George McCorquodale & Co and Webb & Hunt, Liverpool 1852

30. Rounded

31. Table 4.6 in Brinley Thomas, 'Britain's Food Supply 1760–1846: the Irish contribution' in *The Industrial Revolution and the Atlantic Economy: selected essays* Routledge, London and New York 1993

32. ibid p.95

33. Railway Commissioners, op.cit, part 1

34. Peter Solar, 'Shipping and economic development in nineteenth-century Ireland', in *Economic History Review* LIX, 4 2006, pp.717–42

35. Rhodes, op.cit

36. Freda Harcourt, 'Charles Wye Williams and Irish steam shipping, 1820–50' in *The Journal of Transport History*, Third Series Vol.13, No.2, September 1992, pp.141–62

37. Railway Commissioners, op.cit, Appendix B, No.6. Drawbacks (discounts) on the Shannon traffic kept growth in income lower than that in tonnage

38. Delany, op.cit, Appendix 4 citing *Thom's Directories*

39. Delany and Bath, op.cit: Appendix 8

40. Shannon Commissioners 11th Report: *Eleventh and Final Report from the Commissioners, Under the Act 2 & 3 Vict c61, for the improvement of the navigation of the River Shannon, Ireland; with an Appendix,* Ordered, by the House of Commons to be Printed, 3 June 1850

41. *Sic*. This figure from the Commissioners' 11th report appears to have been taken straight from their 2nd report

42. Shannon Commissioners, 11th Report, op.cit

43. ibid

44. Shepherd, op.cit

45. Cormac Ó Gráda, *Ireland: a new economic history 1780–1939,* Clarendon Press, Oxford 1994. Table 11.1 from Michael Turner, 'Agricultural Output and Productivity in Post-Famine Ireland', 1991

46. John O'Donovan, *The Economic History of Live Stock in Ireland,* Cork University Press, 1940

47. Weld, op.cit

48. MGWR advert in *The Freeman's Journal* 8 November 1848

49. Joseph Tatlow, *Fifty years of Railway Life in England, Scotland and Ireland,* The Railway Gazette, London 1920

Chapter 3: Some Royal Canal carriers

50. *The Freeman's Journal,* 30 January 1846

51. *I. Slater's National Commercial Directory of Ireland: including, in addition to the trades' lists, alphabetical directories of Dublin, Belfast, Cork and Limerick. To which are added, classified directories of the important English towns of Manchester, Liverpool, Birmingham, Sheffield, Leeds and Bristol; and, in Scotland, those of Glasgow and Paisley. Embellished with a large new map of Ireland, faithfully depicting the lines of railways in operation or in progress, engraved on steel.* I. Slater, Manchester, 1846

52. *Thom's Irish Almanac and Official Directory with the Post Office Dublin City and County Directory, for the year 1850,* Alexander Thom, Dublin; Longman, Brown, Green, and Longmans, London; Adam and Charles Black, Edinburgh 1850

53. I note however that Appendix C in Peter Clarke, *The Royal Canal: the complete story,* Elo Publications, Dublin 1992 lists 'Boat Owners operating on the Royal Canal 1826 to 1847' including four Royal Canal Company boats as well as four Midland Great Western Railway boats.

54. *The Freeman's Journal,* 3 October 1839

55. Railway Commissioners, Appendix B, No.6 in *Second report of the Commissioners appointed to consider and recommend a general system of Railways for Ireland,* HMSO, 1838 [Session 1837–8, Cmd 145, vol.35, p.449]

56. Clarke, Appendix C, op.cit

57. *The Freeman's Journal,* 23 February 1853

58. Railway Commissioners, Appendix B, no.6, op.cit

59. This example is from *The Freeman's Journal* of 14 April 1838 but the same phrase is found in many adverts throughout the period

60. Clarke, Appendix C, op.cit

61. Ruth Delany and Ian Bath, *Ireland's Royal Canal 1789–2009*, The Lilliput Press, Dublin 2010

62. Railway Commissioners, Appendix B, no.6, op.cit

63. ibid

64. Mary John Knott, *Two Months at Kilkee* (first published 1836), Clasp Press, Ennis 1997

65. MGWR half-yearly meeting 28 March 1851 in *The Freeman's Journal*, 29 March 1851

66. Delany and Bath, op.cit

67. Clarke, op.cit

68. 8 & 9 Vict c42

69. *The Freeman's Journal*, 25 June 1852

70. *The Freeman's Journal*, 15 August 1853. Coincidentally, shortly afterwards the company decided to cease contracting out the haulage of its railway trains: the directors' report to the half-yearly meeting on 14 March 1854, reported in *The Freeman's Journal* of 15 March 1855, said that 'Since the last half-yearly meeting the directors have resumed the haulage of the trains.'

71. *The Freeman's Journal*, 29 November 1853

72. *The Freeman's Journal*, 23 September 1854

73. *Thom's Irish Almanac and Official Directory of the United Kingdom for the year 1857*, Alexander Thom and Sons, Dublin; Longman, Brown, Green, Longmans, and Roberts, London; Adam and Charles Black, Edinburgh 1857

74. *Dublin Evening Mail*, 23 March 1861

75. I take it that these comparisons are made with the previous year's figures for the same half-year period.

76. MGWR half-yearly meeting, 19 Sept. 1861 in *The Freeman's Journal*, 20 September 1861

77. *The Freeman's Journal*, 24 January 1863

78. *Dublin Evening Mail*, 19 March 1863

79. *The Freeman's Journal*, 18 September 1863

80. op.cit

81. Clarke Appendix C, op.cit

82. *The Irish Times*, 8 September 1876

83. *Sic*: it was actually a resumption

84. *The Freeman's Journal*, 11 September 1876

85. ibid

Chapter 4: Romance brought up the nine-fifteen

86. *The Freeman's Journal*, 22 August 1845

87. *The Freeman's Journal*, 25 March 1846

88. 'Return to an Order of the Honourable The House of Commons, dated 3 March 1854, for ... Copies of any instructions issued by the Treasury relative to the security of [loans under the Act of 12 & 13 Vict c62 (Athlone and Galway Railway)]' in House of Commons *Accounts and Papers: thirty-six volumes —(19)— Ireland. Session 31 January – 12 August 1854 Vol LVII. 1854*

89. ibid

90. *The Freeman's Journal*, 28 September 1850

91. *The Freeman's Journal*, 2 March 1877

92. *The Freeman's Journal*, 5 March 1886

93. *The Freeman's Journal*, 15 July 1850

94. http://www.measuringworth.com It also gives the economic status value of £135,000 in 1850 as £161,500,000 in 2013 and its economic power as £373,800,000 in 2013

95. *The Daily News*, 11 April 1856

96. I cite several newspaper reports but, on each topic, there are many more to be found in the online British Newspaper Archive http://www.britishnewspaperarchive.co.uk.

97. Vera Hughes, *The Strange Story of Sarah Kelly*, [no publisher's name; ISBN 0 9513994 0 3], 1988. On some matters, the newspaper reports of the time – despite their evident weaknesses – add detail and sometimes suggest conclusions other than those reached by Vera Hughes and by a television programme broadcast in 2006

98. Peter Clarke, *The Royal Canal: the complete story*, Elo Publications, Dublin 1992; Ruth Delany and Ian Bath, *Ireland's Royal Canal 1789–2009*, The Lilliput Press, Dublin 2010; W.E. [Ernie] Shepherd, *The Midland Great Western Railway of Ireland: an illustrated history*, Midland Publishing Limited, East Shilton 1994

99. The *Caledonian Mercury*, 26 April 1819 has a brief report; there is a longer account in the *Chester Courant, and Anglo-Welsh Gazette*, 4 May 1819 and the *Lancaster Gazette*, 15 May 1819

100. *The Daily News*, 11 April 1856

101. Charles Phillips, *Curran and his Contemporaries*, Harper & Brothers, New York 1862. He described an Irish attorney as 'a perfect, but, indeed, a very favourable specimen of a class of men now quite extinct in Ireland ... They were a kind of compound of

the rack-rent squire and the sharp law practitioner – careless and craving – extravagant and usorious – honorable and subtle – just as their education or their nature happened to predominate at the moment'.

102. *Sussex Advertiser*, 15 April 1856

103. *The Freeman's Journal*, 3 March 1846

104. Hughes, op.cit

105. Hughes, op.cit and *The Freeman's Journal* 18 April 1853

106. Hughes, op.cit

107. Court report in *The Freeman's Journal*, 3 March 1846

108. Hughes, op.cit

109. *Liverpool Mercury*, 17 January 1851

110. *Cork Examiner*, 12 July 1852

111. *Cheltenham Chronicle*, 24 February 1853

112. *London Standard*, 26 September 1853

113. *Royal Cornwall Gazette*, 15 January 1858

114. This account is based on many newspaper accounts, including reports of the inquest

115. *The Freeman's Journal*, 19 November 1856

116. *Royal Cornwall Gazette*, 15 January 1858

117. See for example http://www.theirishstory.com/2011/01/07/madame-mistress-and-martinet-the-life-of-sarah-kelly/

118. *Belfast News-Letter*, 17 April 1876

119. *The Freeman's Journal*, 8 September 1876

Chapter 5: Mallet's Insistent Pontoon

120. Railway Commissioners, Appendix B, No.6 in *Second report of the Commissioners appointed to consider and recommend a general system of Railways for Ireland*, HMSO 1838 [Session 1837–8, Cmd 145, vol.35 p.449]

121. W.E. (Ernie) Shepherd, *The Midland Great Western Railway of Ireland: an illustrated history*, Midland Publishing Limited 1994

122. Maurice Craig, *Dublin 1660–1860: a social and architectural history*, Allen Figgis Ltd, Dublin 1969

123. Robert Mallet 'Description of the Insistent Pontoon Bridge, at the Dublin Terminus of the Midland Great Western Railway of Ireland' in Institution of Civil Engineers *Minutes of the Proceedings*, vol.9, issue 1850 01, January 1850, pp.344–52

124. ibid

125. *The Chambers Dictionary*, 10th ed, Edinburgh 2006

126. https://en.wikipedia.org/wiki/Gutta-percha checked 9 June 2014

127. Ruth Delany and Ian Bath, *Ireland's Royal Canal 1789–2009*, The Lilliput Press, Dublin 2010

128. *The Irish Times*, 13 September 1933

129. T. Doyle, *Luas Broombridge: Advance Archaeological Testing at Broadstone: Assessment Report* (Licence 10E0090), Headland Archaeology Ltd for the Railway Procurement Agency 2010

130. T. Bolger, *Report on Archaeological Slit Trenches at Broadstone – Future Luas Works – Luas Broombridge (BXD), Dublin* (Licence 12E0310 [ext]), Rubicon Heritage Ltd for the Railway Procurement Agency 2013

131. F. Myles, *Advance Archaeological Excavations, Broadstone Canal and Harbour, Luas Cross City, Dublin* (Licence 14E0018) Archaeology and Built Heritage Ltd for the Railway Procurement Agency (forthcoming)

Chapter 6: Steam in the 1870s

132. Samuel Lewis, *A Topographical Dictionary of Ireland, comprising the several counties, cities, boroughs, corporate, market, and post towns, parishes, and villages, with historical and statistical descriptions; embellished with engravings of the arms of the cities, bishopricks, corporate towns, and boroughs; and of the seals of the several municipal corporations: with an appendix, describing the electoral boundaries of the several boroughs, as defined by the Act of the 2d & 3d of William IV*, S. Lewis & Co, London 1837

133. W.E. (Ernie) Shepherd, *The Midland Great Western Railway of Ireland: an illustrated history*, Midland Publishing Ltd, Leicester 1994

134. *The Freeman's Journal*, 23 September 1870

135. *The Irish Times*, 22 September 1871. The account of the meeting in the same day's issue of *The Freeman's Journal* does not cover this topic

136. Peter Clarke, *The Royal Canal: The Complete Story*, Elo Publications, Dublin 1992

137. Ruth Delany and Ian Bath, *Ireland's Royal Canal 1789–2009*, in association with Waterways Ireland, Lilliput Press, Dublin 2010

138. Ruth Delany, *The Shannon Navigation*, Lilliput Press, Dublin 2008

139. *The Irish Times*, 8 September 1876

140. ibid. *The Freeman's Journal* of the same date gives a much shorter account

141. Sir Ralph Cusack at the half-yearly meeting of the MGWR on 1 March 1877 quoted in *The Freeman's Journal* on March 1877. The wharf in question was outside the Guinness brewery, just downstream of Kingsbridge/Heuston station on the river Liffey; the steamer was carrying the porter downstream to the Royal Canal [Spencer] Dock

142. *The Irish Times* and *The Freeman's Journal*, 11 October 1877 and later

143. Sir Ralph Cusack at the half-yearly meeting of the MGWR on 7 March 1878 quoted in *The Freeman's Journal* on 8 March 1878

144. ibid

145. *The Irish Times*, 26 July 1884

146. *The Freeman's Journal*, 20 September and 1 October 1884

147. Notice dated 6 March 1886 in *The Freeman's Journal*, 12 and 13 March 1886; a similar advert appeared on 31 May and 19 June 1886

148. Report of the Grand Canal Company's half-yearly meeting 20 August 1887 in *The Freeman's Journal*, 22 August 1887

149. *The Irish Times*, 17 May 1875

150. *The Freeman's Journal*, 25 January 1877

151. ibid

152. *The Freeman's Journal*, 29 January 1877. The Irish mile, officially abandoned in 1824, was roughly 1¼ statute miles, about 2 km

153. *The Irish Times*, 15 February 1877

154. *The Freeman's Journal*, 30 April 1877

155. Chairman's address to MGWR half-yearly meeting 1 March 1877 reported in *The Freeman's Journal*, 2 March 1877

156. *The Freeman's Journal*, 18 June 1877

157. *The Irish Times*, 16 August 1877 and *The Freeman's Journal*, 24 August 1877

158. Adverts in *The Freeman's Journal* on several dates in September 1877

159. Chairman's address to MGWR half-yearly meeting 6 September 1877 reported in *The Freeman's Journal*, 7 September 1877

160. *The Irish Times*, 13 October 1877 and *The Freeman's Journal*, 10 October 1877; it appeared again in the *Journal* on 29 October 1877, 9 November 1877, 28 December 1877, 9 January 1878 and 21 January 1878

161. The earliest MGWR adverts were dated 11 October 1877

162. Editorial in *The Freeman's Journal*, 10 Oct. 1877. Fishbourne's responded the next day

163. Information from Alison Leighton, whose October 2010 thesis, *Hayes of Stony Stratford: An Inland Boatyard in the late 19th and early 20th Centuries* was submitted towards the MA in Maritime History at the University of Greenwich/ Greenwich Maritime Institute

Chapter 7: Royal Canal bridges in Dublin

164. V.T.H. and D.R. Delany, *The Canals of the South of Ireland*, David & Charles, Newton Abbot 1966, p.234

165. http://maps.osi.ie/publicviewer/#V1,588882,739883,0,10 checked June 2014

166. *The Freemans Journal*, 12 April 1873

167. *The Irish Times*, 14 March 1873

168. Michael Corcoran, *Through Streets Broad and Narrow: a history of Dublin trams*, Midland Publishing, Leicester 2000, pp.20–21

169. *The Irish Times*, 12 October 1875

170. The fact that it is not named after a director of the Royal Canal would indicate that it was built later

171. Louis O'Flaherty, *Drumcondra and its Environs*, Drumcondra Publications, Dublin, 2011, p.21

172. http://roots.swilson.info/dublin1818/DublinCityPlan1818.html accessed 23:23 on 22 February 2013

173. http://roots.swilson.info/DublinCity1836.html accessed 23:23 on 22 February 2013

174. The normal practice, which can still be seen in houses of a similar era, is that a three-storey house would be built with the lower floor half-way below street level with access steps starting at road level rising to a front door at first floor level

175. Gunniting is a process whereby liquid concrete is sprayed onto a structure to provide structural stability upon the setting of the concrete. It also makes non-destructive archaeology difficult!

176. O'Flaherty, op.cit, p.101

177. Corcoran, op.cit, p.94

178. O'Flaherty, op.cit, p.6

179. Peter O'Keeffe and Tom Simington, *Irish Stone Bridges: history and heritage*, Irish Academic Press, Dublin 1991, pp.34–5

180. When the Bill to allow the building of the Liffey Line was passing through Parliament, it was noted that the MGWR had proposed to cross Mayor Street and Sherriff Street by level crossing but that the Board of Trade had objected and wanted bridges (*The Freemans*

Journal, 23 July 1859). As it happened, as Mayor Street was already severed by the Royal Canal, neither bridge nor level crossing was built at Mayor Street. The road remained severed until the building of the Luas line extension to the Point Depot. Sherriff Street got a fixed bridge over the railway and a lifting bridge over the canal.

181. *The Irish Times*, 29 October 1863

Chapter 8: Watson's Double Canal Boat

182. Brian J. Goggin, 'Charles Wye Williams and the "Bendy Boat"', Railway & Canal Historical Society *Waterway History Research Group, Occasional Paper 82*, 12 March 2011

183. Charles Wye Williams, Assoc Inst CE 'Description of the "Nonsuch" Iron Passage Boat plying on the Limerick navigation, between that place and Killaloe', in *Proceedings of the Institution of Civil Engineers*, 1 (1840), p.28

184. ibid

185. 'Steam Navigation on the Shannon' from *Saunders's News Letter* in *The Mechanics' Magazine*, vol.xxxv, no.953, (13 Nov. 1841) and no.954, (20 Nov. 1841)

186. 'List of Irish patents granted in March 1838' in *The Mechanics' Magazine*, no.768, 28 April 1838

187. The *Mechanics' Magazine*, vol.xxxII, no.855, 28 December 1839

188. P.J.G. Ransom mentioned the existence of the drawing in *The Archaeology of the Transport Revolution 1750–1850*, World's Work Ltd, Tadworth 1984. The Canal & River Trust is the successor to British Waterways

189. 'Steam Navigation on the Shannon', op.cit

190. 'Steam Power on Canals' in *Minutes of Proceedings of the Institution of Civil Engineers*, vol.xxvi, 1866–67 reproduced on the Steamers Historical website with the Institute's permission:
http://www.steamershistorical.co.uk/steam%20power%20on%20canals.1867.23152.pdf

191. 'Steam Power on Canals', op.cit

192. 'Steam Navigation on the Shannon', op.cit

193. ibid

194. 'Steam Power on Canals', op.cit

195. 'Steam Navigation on the Shannon', op.cit

196. From its occasional references to 'British miles', it is possible that *Saunders's* used Irish miles by default. One Irish mile was about 1¼ British (statute) miles or about 2 km, so six Irish miles equalled 7½ statute miles. The Irish mile was legally abolished in 1824 but continued in popular use for some time thereafter.

197. 'Steam Power on Canals', op.cit

198. ibid

199. 'Steam Navigation on the Shannon', op.cit

200. Roseanne Dunne, 'No 25 Fitzwilliam Place', *Dublin Historical Record*, vol.49, no.1 (Spring 1996), pp.59–63, Old Dublin Society. Article Stable
URL: http://www.jstor.org/stable/30101133

201. Brian J. Goggin, 'The Mahmoudié mystery', Railway & Canal Historical Society, *Waterway History Research Group Occasional Paper 106*, 6 April 2014

202. Freda Harcourt, 'The High Road to India: The P&O Company and the Suez Canal, 1840–1874', in *International Journal of Maritime History*, vol.xxII, no.2, Dec. 2010, pp.19–72 http://ijh.sagepub.com/content/22/2/19.citation

203. Halford Lancaster Hoskins, *British Routes to India*, Longmans, Green and Co, New York, London, Toronto 1928

204. Cavendish Philatelic Auctions http://tinyurl.com/qx2r0a3 Auction 757 item 323: 'Letters of appreciation for Waghorn's services in Egypt'

205. *Cornwall Royal Gazette*, 4 June 1841 at the British Newspaper Archive http://www.britishnewspaperarchive.co.uk/

206. *The Hampshire Advertiser and Salisbury Guardian*, 11 December 1841 at the British Newspaper Archive http://www.britishnewspaperarchive.co.uk/